Finding Her Sweet Spot

by William Wright

Copyright © 2013 by Wright Way Publishing, LLC

All rights reserved. In accordance with U.S. Copyright act of 1976, the scanning, uploading and electronic sharing of any part of this book without the permission of the publisher is unlawful and theft of the authors intellectual property. If you would like to use material from this book (other than for review), prior written permission must be obtained by contacting the publisher at customerservice@wrightwaypublishing.com.

Published by Wright Way Publishing, LLC

10645 N. Tatum Blvd, Suite 200-370

Phoenix, AZ 85028

The publisher is not responsible for any websites (or their content) that are not owned by publisher.

First Edition: December 2013

ISBN-13:
978-0615933177 (Wright Way Publishing, LLC)

ISBN-10:
0615933173

DEDICATIONS

In Loving Memory:

Bella Rosenberg – A remarkable woman and a beautiful soul. Her love and support for her family was immeasurable.

And

Scott Zaffrin – A friend, brother and mentor. He was an authentic "free spirit." He channeled positive energy, success and happiness to everyone around him.

Chapters

Acknowledgments 1

Introduction 3

Step 1 – You Met Her Where? - Meeting a Woman
9

Step 2 – Is She or Is She Not - The First Date
27

Step 3 – Reach Out and Touch Someone - Phone Calls and Texts **41**

Step 4 – The Writing on the Wall – Beginning Dating Rituals **49**

Step 5 – The Inquisition - Meeting Her Friends and Family **67**

Step 6 – Woo Hoo! - Sex For The First Time
75

Step 7 – Practice Makes Perfect – Spending Time Together **87**

Step 8 - At the Sound of the Bell Come Out Disagreeing **99**

Step 9 – The Merger – Moving in Together
109

Step 10 – Don't Pop the Question, Plan the Question **121**

Step 11 –And They Lived Happily Ever After Far From the End **127**

Step 12 – Appreciate Your Life - Share the Love
139

Conclusion 145

WILLIAM WRIGHT

ACKNOWLEDGMENTS

I would like thank all my very dear friends and family who have supported me, shared their lives and enhanced my life through the years. Those that were expressly responsible for directing me on the positive and successful path I currently follow; you have my deepest gratitude and love.

I would also like to thank my amazing editor Nicole Hatton. Her hard work and encouragement made it possible to share the concepts in this book easily and effectively. We hope it will help thousands, if not millions, of people to achieve outstanding relationships and substantial happiness in their lives.

WILLIAM WRIGHT

Introduction

> ***Sweet Spot:*** *the best possible place or combination of factors*

No matter what stage of a relationship you are in, it is never too early or too late to start wooing your woman. Whether you are eighteen or eighty, and looking to meet someone, or already have a girlfriend or a wife, you can still learn techniques to improve your relationship. Even if you have been married for fifty years, you can make the woman you love fall in love with you all over again.

I'm sitting at a big table with a group of buddies: Bob, Jeff, Labron, Doug and Javier. They all have different styles, personalities and backgrounds. We are at *Maxwell's*: a vibrant restaurant that bustles with patrons and friendly wait staff. Popular music creates an upbeat atmosphere, but we can still talk easily. We are sharing our thoughts while interjecting mild, friendly digs at each other. Occasionally there are outbursts of laughter, pointing and elbow poking. Our conversation has already touched on sports, our jobs, politics, cars and what we did last weekend. Inevitably, the conversation turns to women...

Bob boasts that he "knows everything" about women, but we don't take him too seriously. He is trying to impress us, but he has too much testosterone and not enough good sense. I also know that no one man knows everything! No one man has all the answers. Mostly because, all women are different! There is no exact science to make a woman fall in love with you. Every woman has her own unique mind, body and spirit.

> ***Woo***: *to seek the favor, affection, or love of, especially with a view to marriage*

The successful methods in this book are guidelines to be adjusted by you, and the woman you are interested in. Finding a woman's sweet spot is not getting a woman to go on a date with you or getting lucky on the first date. Finding a woman's sweet spot is the art of wooing a woman, getting a woman to continue dating you, while building a happy, loving and long lasting relationship. This is not a book about how to get more women to sleep with you. It is, however, a book about human nature (his and hers), psychology, neurology and learning more about yourself and the woman you are going to woo.

We all learn from what we personally experience. We learn about relationship building from the relationships we observe as we are growing up. This can be a positive experience or a negative one. Certain basic life skills we are never taught at home or in school. As a child, you learned from watching the behaviors of your parents and other adults. But realize their way might not have been the most effective way. They were not intentionally trying to steer you wrong. They were teaching you what they were taught by someone else. Your childhood friends taught you how to interact with other kids, and this same dynamic continued into adolescence. We all remember our first kiss, first date, first time having sex, and of course our first time having sex with someone else (woo hoo). What did we learn? Who were we learning from? Was someone trying to impress you? Was it someone who wanted something from you? Perhaps it was someone who was genuinely trying to be caring and supportive, but didn't really know how. Relationship building is a learnable skill. You have to be willing to look inside yourself and find out what your beliefs are. Do they help you or hold you back? You have to decide what type of relationship you want and possibly change your current beliefs to help you get there. You need to continually grow as an individual in order to grow within a relationship. Your inner belief system affects all areas of your life, not just your relationships. Within all areas of your life where you want to achieve success, make sure your inner beliefs match your goals.

Your inner beliefs are just the story that you tell yourself. You tell yourself a story every day, and it's about you. It is your beliefs that are stored in a file cabinet in your brain. Your story could be positive or negative. The story is based on the individual experiences in your unique life. It is based on what you have heard, learned and deemed to be true. It may be correct or could be totally false. The great reality here is that you get to decide. You get to write your own story. You get to decide what you believe to be true and positive in your life. You get to decide the person you want to be. Perhaps someone treated you as if you didn't deserve love and success. That doesn't make it true. It only means someone else has imposed their story on you. They told you the story they believe to be true about themselves. You can decide that you are kind, add value to others people's lives, and deserve all the love and success the universe has to offer. Fortunately, you get to decide the direction of your story and your life based on the positive ideas that work for you.

I wrote this book because I am one of the guys at the table. Not long ago I was the last person you would have expected to write a book about relationships. When I started working at the age of twelve, I was focused on two things: sex and money. Not that unusual for a young boy. Throughout my teenage years, I developed a very effective skillset to aid me in my pursuit of women. For two decades I often spent time with more than one women in a week. There were times when I made a commitment to one woman, in which case I was monogamous. I never cheated in a relationship or practiced deception, but there came a point when I wanted more. The "More" was having a committed relationship with a woman you care for who satisfies your soul. This amazing woman satisfies your needs for companionship, sex, love, sharing your life and a best friend. Allow us to help you to win the heart of the woman that makes you want "More."

Now imagine you are sitting at the table with us. Grab a drink and some snacks, because we are going to share with you the secrets we have learned and share our life experiences. I also look forward to hearing about the new insights and secrets you learn. I hope you will share your thoughts after you have finished hanging out with us at www.findinghersweetspot.com.

Names, dates, places and specific information have been changed in this book to protect the innocent from embarrassment, as well as their girlfriends and wives.

WILLIAM WRIGHT

Step 1 – You Met Her Where? - Meeting a Woman

"Winners make a habit of manufacturing their own positive expectations in advance of the event."

- Brian Tracy / Motivational Speaker and Author

To meet the woman of your dreams, you don't have to be wealthy, man pretty (like a male model), have an IQ of 180, be hung like a porn star or have muscles like a body builder. Nor do you need to be a professional athlete, an international spy, or a successful politician. You don't have to live in a mansion or drive a Ferrari. These types of men make up about one percent of the male population on the planet. This one percent is not dating one hundred percent of the women on the planet. So who are the women dating? They are dating us! The average man that is extraordinary unto himself. If you don't feel extraordinary, then we just need to boost your confidence so that you can understand and believe in yourself. Let's take an example like Don Juan. In the original Spanish tragedy, Don Juan's attractive qualities were his vitality, his courage, and his sense of humor. This fictional character's name is automatically associated with a man who could sleep with any woman he wanted. Even though he is fictional, I imagine he would have had to meet, talk to and impress those women before sleeping with them. He seduced them with his heart, his words and his actions.

If you are chronically shy and introverted, these concepts still apply to you. You might have to work a little harder to take the steps, but you have to push yourself little by little. Remember the story of the Tortoise and the Hare? You don't have to be the fastest in the race; you just have to finish it. According to Dr. Bernardo J. Carducci of the Shyness Research Institute, shyness has three components:

1) Excessive Self-Consciousness – you are highly aware of yourself, particularly in social situations.
2) Excessive Negative Self-Evaluation – you tend to see yourself negatively.
3) Excessive Negative Self-Preoccupation– you tend to pay too much attention to all the things you are doing "wrong" when you are around other people.

Shyness is a debilitating condition for many men. It prevents them from functioning in social situations, from voicing their real concerns, and most sadly, from approaching the woman of their dreams. The truth is that many shy men are exactly the kind of guy women look for. But since they're too timid, women get left with the swaggering jerks they always complain about, but seem to date more often.

Top 10 Ways to Overcome Shyness

1) **Practice for a friend** - A big factor in shyness is the fear of rejection. Eliminate this factor by approaching and picking up a woman for your friend. Since your own ego isn't at stake, you'll be less inhibited in your approach. You'll see it's no big deal and will want to pick up for yourself next time.

2) **Take baby steps** - Treat dating like a 12-step program. Start with a smile; show everyone (not just the hot babes) that you're friendly and approachable. On following days, move up to saying "Hi." A few days after that, engage in small talk. As you gradually open yourself up to people, you'll see it's not as hard as you thought. If you make a blunder, forget about it. Most people are more forgiving than you think.

3) **Don't sexualize women so much** - When you talk to a woman, don't view her as a sexual trophy, but as a person like yourself. Keeping things purely sexual will get in the way of your approach. And women can sense when a guy is just after sex.

4) **Don't put women on a pedestal** - Don't attach any special significance to the woman you talk to. If you act like she's too good for you, she'll likely start thinking that as well. See her as a human being with all the flaws and qualities of the average person. Talking one-on-one is much nicer than talking down

to or up to another person.

5) **Adjust your expectations** - When you talk to a woman, don't expect an end goal; just go with the flow. You'll be amazed at how much easier things get when you don't think you have to accomplish something by the end. If you keep your cool, the rewards will present themselves naturally.

6) **Don't take things personally** - If you want to succeed in the game of romance, you can't take every comment, insinuation or joke that a woman might throw your way personally. People sometimes say things they don't mean. You'll have nothing to be self-conscious about if nothing bothers you. However, sometimes people do make inappropriate comments, in which case, you should definitely point out your discontent with the conversation.

7) **Learn to listen** - Don't do all the talking. Let the woman you are talking to talk about herself for a while. Most people love to have someone to talk to who is a good listener. Ask open-ended questions and just sit back and listen. If the conversation lulls, have new questions ready.

8) **Talk to a lot of people** - Don't be afraid to talk to everyone you meet, from the old lady doing her groceries to the bank teller. Practice makes perfect. Most people secretly desire communication with others, so your friendliness will usually be welcome. And if it's not, brush it off. Remember, you are not the only shy one.

FINDING HER SWEET SPOT

9) **Don't fear rejection** - Great boxers go in the ring knowing there's a chance they'll lose. Similarly, you can't expect to succeed every time. Nothing is one hundred percent, so view every encounter with a woman as a positive learning experience. The trick here is to not be self-conscious. Shyness and hesitation occur when you think about your flaws. Instead, focus your thoughts entirely on the woman you're talking to. You'll forget about your jitters and she'll be flattered by the attention.

10) **Get out and socialize** - Join activities in which you're always interacting with people, such as the gym, meet-up groups or a hobby club. These situations are highly social by their nature. Furthermore, they give you more opportunities to meet interesting women.

If you meet a woman you are interested in, your first thought is "I have interest in her." It could be an intellectual or sexual attraction, but a part of your brain immediately fires and sends you this message. Your next thought should be "I am going to speak to her." Too often men think of a hundred reasons why she would not talk to or go out with them. Here is your chance to possibly meet the woman of your dreams. Her brain could be sending her the same message: "I have interest in him," yet your fear comes up with excuses as you watch her walk away. Now you wonder--What if I had just said "Hi"? Women like a confident man! *Confident*, not cocky or arrogant. There is a huge difference. If you are truly looking to meet the woman of your dreams you might have to fake that feeling of confidence until you authentically feel it. And inevitably you will. You will have to talk to her. No passing notes to each other like you did in grade school. One way to build your confidence is to look at yourself in the mirror every morning and tell yourself one of your better qualities (I am good-hearted, handsome, smart, a hard worker, etc…) and a meaningful goal you would like to accomplish this day. Setting and accomplishing small goals daily will help to build your self-confidence in all areas of your life. It may sound corny to talk to yourself in the mirror, but if it works, better corny and successful. And it works! Plus, I'm sure you have said weirder things to yourself in the mirror. I know I have.

Another good way to work toward your goal of meeting the woman of your dreams is to use the law of attraction. That is, what you focus on is what you get. Most successful people use this technique to acquire what they want in life. The first step is to be absolutely clear about what you want. Writing down in very specific detail what you want in a woman can help you find her. Include hair color, eye color, height, skin tone, body type, etc… any physical characteristic that you want. The more details the better. Then write down what she is like: Is she sweet? Funny? Caring? Sensual? Demure? Outgoing? Be specific. You have a much better chance of finding her if you create a clear picture in your mind of who you're looking for. Along with your description, add a date to achieve your goal of meeting the woman of your dreams. Also, set a realistic time frame in which to meet her. By including a specific date you expect to achieve your goal, you can monitor your progress and gauge how much more work is necessary to complete your task. As personal success writer Napoleon Hill once said, "A goal is a dream with a deadline."

Get into the habit of practicing your conversational and social skills. You can and should start conversations with total strangers. It's as simple as saying hello to a stranger standing next to you. We have opportunities every day to interact with people. I am continuously amazed by how often people will stand in line and pretend not to notice the other people standing around them. You will be surprised at the number of people who will engage in a conversation with you if you just make the first move and say "Hi" or "Good morning." To start honing your new social skills you can make it a habit to start a conversation with at least one new person a day.

The purpose of the exercise is to become comfortable starting and continuing a conversation with people you don't know. Beyond dating, this skill can be very helpful in many areas of your life. Keep in mind that most people like to talk about themselves. When given the chance, they will usually take it. A great way to engage someone is to ask open-ended, probing questions about them. For example, instead of saying, "Do you like this song?" You can ask, "What are some of your favorite bands?" An open-ended question can't be answered with a single word. When people have to elaborate, they are coaxed into further conversation. And this usually leads to more open-ended questions. As this interaction goes on, they are slowly sharing personal information about themselves and becoming more comfortable with you. People feel bonded to other people when they can comfortably share their personal thoughts and experiences. By finding things you have in common, they will feel more connected to you.

Asking open-ended, probing questions is actually a sales technique used by the most successful sales people to learn more about you. You really don't even realize they are doing it. They use it to gain information about you, build your trust, and make you feel comfortable talking to them. They will continue to ask only questions for which you have to explain an answer until they have an educated idea of what you might be interested in. If they are a good salesperson, they will evaluate all the information you have given them and amaze you by showing you just the product you are looking for. You will now feel like they understand you and have your best interests in mind.

You can use this technique to find out more about the woman you just met and to decide if you want to ask her out on a date. Consider it a quick interview. I have used this simple technique of saying "Hi" to a woman in a parking lot and then had the opportunity to ask her questions about the store I saw her coming out of. This one word coupled with some open-ended questions led to a twenty minute conversation and a date the next night. Of course, not all people will respond so eagerly. Some folks will just say "Hi" back and turn away. And some will just ignore you. That's acceptable. You just learned that this is not a person you would want to invest time talking to anyway. Don't be discouraged by people who are negative or suspicious of you just because you are friendly. You will become a happier, more socially adjusted person for it.

Eventually one of the women you talk to as you are practicing your social skills will be the woman you described for yourself.

Your energy and emotional state influences the energy around you. If you are calm and happy when interacting with others, they will feel comfortable and respond the same way. If you are anxious, agitated or have a bad attitude, again others will respond the same. People can sense confidence and warmth, as well as fear and aggression. If someone walked up to you at a steady pace with a smile on their face, you would think they were coming over to talk with you. On the other hand, if someone walked up to you quickly, with an angry look on their face, your brain would automatically prepare for conflict. The best way to calm an excited and agitated person is for you to be calm yourself. When you approach people, be relaxed. Think positive thoughts. If you are kind, warm and friendly, people will typically exhibit similar behavior. Any negative thoughts you have will make you appear apprehensive and they will instantly feel uncomfortable. Your mind can easily conjure a hundred different reasons not to talk to someone. Focus on the positive motivations and outcomes for meeting someone-- your happiness. Try becoming more of a positive thinker in general. If you portray a positive attitude in all areas of your life, people will comment that you seem to be a happy person. And best of all, you will feel happier.

For some people starting a conversation with a stranger is very difficult. Fear of rejection is a very common phobia. People fear that if they start a conversation with someone, and the person does not engage or cuts them short, then the person is rejecting them. When you start a conversation or talk to someone new, you have no idea what other unrelated events they may have dealt with that day. Maybe they are just having a bad day. There are a thousand reasons why someone might not feel like having a conversation. Don't take it personally, and remember your goal is to meet people who *do* want to talk with you. So no matter what happens, continue to talk to new people every day. Besides, they are strangers, so even if you accidentally said the most bizarre things, and they turned and walked away from you thinking you are just insane, it doesn't matter. You will never see them again anyway. So you have absolutely nothing to lose by trying. Just keep thinking positive thoughts.

There is only one scenario you can be sure of-- you will not find a woman by staying at home alone. Jeff shouts, "What if I'm on an Internet dating website?" with a smirk on his face. That is a whole different ball game and we will talk about that shortly. But for the moment, I am referring to getting out of the house and being around people. Dating success is based on percentages. If you don't ask out at least one woman, your odds of getting a date are zero percent! If you go on one date and decide she is nice but not what you're looking for, you might feel discouraged. But if you do not ask out another woman, your odds of finding the right woman for you are zero percent again! It's like baseball averages. The more times you go up to bat, the more chances you have to hit the ball. You might strike out more, but you will also hit more home runs. You will meet many women in your life. You will date a percentage of those women. A smaller percentage of them will want a relationship with you. You will fall in love with an even smaller percentage of those women. Then you will find "The One." Some very lucky people find the right one very quickly. Others have to look a little harder. But you still have to continue your search. Think of dating as the fairy tale <u>Goldilocks and the Three Bears</u>. Sometimes you have to figure out what you don't like before you find what you do like. The key is to Never Give Up. That goes for any goal in life you want to achieve. Whether it's dating, building a successful career, owning your dream home, driving your dream car, or achieving spiritual enlightenment, you must work at your goals with perseverance until you achieve them. Regularly revisit your detailed description of the woman you want to meet (as well as any other goals you set for yourself).

   I recently visited a shop to have an alarm installed on my truck. When I got there, I was pleasantly surprised to see a very attractive woman working there. At first I thought she was the receptionist, but as we were talking I realized that she was the installer. She asked me some basic questions (she was very professional) and then began to work on my truck. After a while, I got thirsty so I decided to walk to a nearby convenience store. The woman was halfway inside my truck, talking to another installer. She was obviously working hard and sweating. I walked over and said, "I'm going to the store for a drink…can I bring one back for either of you?" The guy barely looking up and said "No thanks," but the girl looked up at me in surprise. She was shocked that I, the customer, was asking her if I could do something for her. She politely declined, but with a huge, sweet smile. When I returned she was nearly finished. She came over to me to explain how the alarm worked and to take payment. After we finished our business transaction, her demeanor changed. She started telling me about the custom work she had done, how she enjoyed being creative, and the work she had done on her own truck. She then asked me if I would like to see her truck which was outside in the parking lot. She showed me the custom work she had done to her truck, and it was amazing! Our conversation gave me a window into her thought process of how she had created this masterpiece of automotive art. I learned why she chose the colors, patterns and designs, along with how she had gotten into this business. And I didn't have to ask a single question! By making a very small, kind gesture to this woman, I gained her trust and instilled in her a desire to connect with me socially. Obviously, this could have been a great dating opportunity if I had not been involved with someone else, but it is also a great life opportunity and a lesson in human behavior. A random act of kindness can go a long way, especially when someone doesn't expect it.

Another great way to meet women is meet-up groups and seminars. These opportunities are superb because you are going to meet a large group of like-minded women. In our Internet age there is a meet up group for any activity you can imagine. There are many websites dedicated to group meet-ups. If you like hiking, biking, motorcycles, eating out, wine tasting, online gaming, Scrabble, traveling, networking, knitting or just hanging out at your local bar, there is a group in your area already doing this! The great part about these meet-up groups is: 1) They are generally mixed: male and female. 2) The women there have the same interests as you. You are already walking into a scenario where starting a conversation is easy. Everyone already has something in common. 3) There are many women, so you can mingle and then choose the one that you are interested in for further conversation. If you feel there is a connection then you can ask to meet her outside the group. 4) You have also now found an entire social group and friends to socialize with in the future. So as well as possibly finding an awesome woman, you might meet some new friends.

Seminars work the same way. Seminars are generally more educational, but the topics can include personal growth, finance, career focus, business opportunities and so much more. Again you are engaging with a group of like-minded people. So once again starting a conversation with that woman who catches your eye is easy. I always enjoy seminars because I consider myself a student for life and always enjoy learning something new while meeting new people. If you are politically inclined, you might seek out a local politician who is looking for volunteers. I never heard of a politician turning down free labor. You could volunteer your time at an SPCA or homeless shelter, or support any cause you feel is worthy of your efforts. These are good opportunities to meet like-minded people, learn something new, help your community and meet a woman with whom you share commonality.

Today we have the Twenty-First century version of the personal ads called online dating. Imagine--people used to put small ads in newspapers with very brief descriptions and no pictures. And this worked? I guess so, since people met and had babies. These days everybody and their sister, mother, and now grandmother has stories about online dating (different sites for every age, background, and interest). It is convenient to meet a woman while sitting in front of your computer in your pajamas, not showered, and eating a bowl of Captain Crunch. As long as you, at some point, make a date, shower, shave, dress appropriately, and go out and meet her. Labron is very proud of himself because he meets women all the time on dating sites. Unfortunately, he *only* meets them on the dating sites. We call him the "Virtual Dating Machine." And yes, he is proud of it, but obviously still single. A conversation online with someone is great, but it's not really a date unless you are both there in person. Labron interjects, "Does video chatting count?" I say, "If that's what makes you happy." But if that makes *you* happy, I don't think this book is for you. Both men and women crave personal interaction. A computer screen cannot replace the human touch. Studies show that the majority of people who have used online dating have met with at least one person who lied or exaggerated on their profile. For example, the picture they had up was ten years old, 6'4 was more like 4'6, weight 165lbs (When? In high school), blonde... (I don't think so) and so on. Be *honest!* There is an unlimited dating pool out there, with someone for everyone. If you portray the real you, your chances of finding someone real are much better. Millions have met their current spouses online. It is just another forum for meeting new people. I also suggest expanding your interests. Matches are made by analyzing data, keyword matches, and complex algorithms. The dating sites only know what you tell them. So if you might have interest in something, check it off! Go for it and expand your horizons. I'm not saying mark down you like skydiving if you're afraid of heights, but if underwater basket weaving is something you think you would like to try, mark it down. It will expand your possibilities of meeting women with the same interests. Remember online dating is a tool, not a crutch. You will eventually have to meet her in person.

Never underestimate the blind date! I have seen people shudder as they tell me they have been fixed up by a friend or family member. What if I don't like her? What if I'm not attracted to her? (Gasp) What if she doesn't like me? What will I tell the person who set up the date if it does not work? What if I have to suffer through the never-ending date from hell? Relax and look at it from a positive perspective; there is actually *less* pressure on a blind date. Yes, I said that! There is nothing invested and nothing at stake. If the date goes well, then great! If not, then you just had a simple, sociable evening. When the date begins, you have an automatic icebreaker. You can talk about the friend you have in common who set up the blind date. The other benefit of accepting a blind date is that there is always a friend, coworker, or family member who knows a single woman. If you let people know you are open to a blind date, you will probably get one. As far as the outcome, everybody involved knows that the outcome of a blind date is so hard to determine, even Vegas won't take odds on it. Most people don't get offended if you didn't have chemistry with the person they set you up with. In most cases they feel bad because they just wanted to make you and the other person happy. On the other hand, if it works out and the lady you meet is wonderful, you owe somebody a bottle of champagne, (or at least a six pack). And they will take credit and brag about it for the rest of your days. Your grandchildren will know them as the matchmaker, *the reason they exist*, the person who introduced Grandma and Grandpa. Either way, it is a win-win situation.

Now it's time to take action! Even a genius needs a plan. So you learned to walk, you learned to ride a bike, now you are learning better ways to date. Try some of these suggestions and come up with some more ideas of your own. But you need to make a plan. You need to decide this is what you want to do and Do It! Write down your plan, research some upcoming events in your area, spread the word that you are single and ready to mingle (sorry had to put that cliché in there somewhere), put the events on your schedule and follow through. Set goals for how many events you would like to attend in a month.

Think positive as you are going out and meeting women. It may take time to meet one that you want to ask out. Remember no game was ever won by a team that expected to lose. Think back to when you were a tiny baby (I don't remember that either). Obviously at some point you were a baby. You were crawling around the living room floor. You propped yourself up, took a step and then fell over. Your parents were proud, as all parents are. You propped yourself up again. You took one step and fell. You tried again, and fell again. You could not get the smile of joy off your face. Do you think your parents said "Oh well, he can't do it. He will just crawl around for the rest of his life"? No! Not an option. Your parents kept propping you up until you took two steps, then three steps and so on until you walked. How many adult people do you know who gave up on learning to walk and now just crawl everywhere? You tried, tried and tried some more until you reached your goal to learn how to walk on your own. Even as a baby, you knew failure was not an option. As children we will go to great lengths to achieve our goals and get what we want. Have you ever been in a mall near a child who wants some ice cream? It truly is a basic instinct: if we don't succeed, try, try again. As adults, we forget that this drive to succeed is our birthright. We develop fears, and give up after a first attempt. So always remember, it's not a question of *will* you meet her, but rather, *when*.

Always keep an open mind. You never know where Ms. Right might show up. Be prepared and practice your conversational skills. Your first date might pop up sooner than you think.

Quick Tip: If you happen to be looking for a new hobby, consider magic. Learning some simple magic tricks that can be performed anywhere is a fantastic ice breaker. People are always drawn to what mystifies them and nobody ever turns down the opportunity to see a fun magic trick. Javier is a nice example of this phenomenon. He practices magic as a hobby and never misses an opportunity to show a trick to a pretty woman. He often does tricks for co-workers, clients and social contacts. When he does his magic tricks, people gather around to watch. Before you know it, he always has an audience

WILLIAM WRIGHT

Step 2 – Is She or Is She Not - The First Date

"How we do anything is how we do everything."

- T. Harv Eker / Motivational Speaker and Author

We have all heard the expression, "You only have one chance to make a first impression." I can't stress enough how true this statement is. On the first date you will be judged on appearance, creativity, actions, conversations, habits, manners, social interaction and everything else you do and don't do. So, "Yeah," it is important. And of course, you will be judging her in the same manner. After all, fair is fair.

Doug quickly jumps in with "I am not judgmental. I would never judge someone's every move like that." I remind him about a first date he went on with a very pretty brunette he had met at work. The plan had been for them to go to dinner and a movie. I remember distinctly him calling me later and telling me that during dinner he had already decided the movie was out of the question and this date was going to end early. As they started their meal with appetizers she apparently started to get food stuck in her teeth. The first time she put her finger to her mouth to use her fingernail to scrape the food from her teeth, he didn't think of anything of it. At the end of the appetizers, when she opened her mouth wider and put her finger into her mouth again to use her nail to scrape between her teeth, he offered to go and get her a toothpick from the front counter. She said, "No thank you, I'm fine." During the meal, as her mouth continuously opened wider and wider, he was picturing having dinner with his family friends while she dug for leftovers in her back molars. By the end of dinner she had at least two fingers in her mouth, reaching for her back teeth and pulling out the chunks of food that had been chewed but didn't quite make it down her throat, until she sucked it off the tips of her fingers and then swallowed them (Eeew). At this point the thought of going to a movie and introducing popcorn into this woman's cavernous oral food traps was more than he could bear. So with a quick trip to the men's room and an unexpected phone call he happened to receive, this date was *ovah*! Now, do I think he was being judgmental? No. He realized quickly this woman had a "habit" that he was not going to be able to live with. I'm sure she was deciding during dinner if he was someone she would want to date again as well.

How you do anything is how you do everything. Think about the effort you put into doing even little things in your life. Are you the type of person who completes a task one hundred percent and to the best of your ability, or do you look for every short cut and stop just when the end is in sight? When you decide you want to make a positive change in your life, do you go for it with everything you've got? Or will you give it some effort until it gets difficult, or you get bored, or it's not happening fast enough? Training yourself to follow through to your desired outcome from the smallest task to a major life transformation takes effort, discipline and awareness. Do you ever take out the garbage but neglect to put a new bag in the trash can? Maybe you load the dishwasher, but leave a few items in the sink for later? Did you decide you want to get in better shape? You went to the gym for a week, decided it was too hard and you didn't look like a model yet, so you quit? Did you ever give up on a relationship that was going well because it required too much work? How you complete even the smallest of tasks is directly proportional to how you complete large tasks. Train yourself to do anything that you do to the best of your ability. Whether it is easy, difficult or just sometimes tedious, discipline yourself to see it through and accomplish the task or goal you set out to achieve. By completing your small goals successfully you will be more likely to push harder to complete your bigger tasks and goals in life. Start becoming aware of how you do anything so you can start doing everything better and achieving all of your life's goals. Whether its relationships, your health or your career, you should always give one hundred percent toward your goals. Put another way, *hold nothing back.*

The purpose of the first date is to determine if this woman is interesting enough for you want to pursue her further, (and vice versa). So always put your best foot forward. It starts before you leave the house. If you are going on a date you should always be freshly showered, shaved and well-groomed overall. Trim all the odd spots that hairs grow out of your body. Trim eyebrow, ear, nose hairs, etc.… And don't forget to trim the toenails. Claws on your feet, not so attractive. If you showered in the morning and have a date at 6 p.m., you should shower again. If you put in that extra effort, the worst thing that could happen is she doesn't notice how especially clean you smell. But believe me she will notice if your deodorant gave up an hour ago.

The sense of smell is a very powerful emotional responder. Whether it is your first date, first anniversary or Fiftieth anniversary, the first time you see your woman on any given day she should want to hug you (to get close) and tell you how good you smell. Our olfactory receptors are directly connected to the limbic system, the most ancient and primitive part of the brain, which is thought to be the base of our emotions. Smells are relayed to the cortex, where 'cognitive' recognition occurs, only after the deepest parts of our brains have been stimulated. So by the time we correctly name a particular scent, say 'vanilla', the scent has already activated the limbic system, triggering more deep-seated emotional responses. Before you can say what the smell is, you already have an emotional response to it. Have you ever held a newborn that needed a diaper change? Need I say more? Studies have proven that for a person who is considered "average" looking, a pleasant fragrance will enhance their appeal and tip the attractiveness scale in their favor. We each have a unique body scent. As you spend time with someone your scent will evoke an emotional response. Some men are cologne guys, some are not. We have found women do respond to the right combination of a man's scent with the right cologne. Nice smelling cologne does not have to be expensive. Try small sample bottles until you find one you like and don't be afraid to ask people's opinions. A woman will frequently compliment you if you smell really good. Just don't be the over-cologned guy. Remember there is a fine line between smelling good and just smelly.

Of course, where you are taking your date will affect what you should be wearing. But no matter where you are going, you should step up your clothes one notch. If you are a biker, and taking her out on your motorcycle, wear a nice fitting, clean T-shirt (I am serious). If you are going somewhere that is a jeans and T-shirt kind of atmosphere, wear a polo shirt. At a jeans and polo shirt event, wear a polo shirt and khakis. Up dress for wherever you are going. You want to make yourself stand out. Remember this is your first impression. When you are in a crowd, you want her to think "Wow, the guy I am with looks nicer than the other guys here." You want her to feel proud to be there with you. It tells her she is important enough for you to go to the trouble of trying to impress her. It also portrays the image that you care about yourself.

Now you look great, smell great and feel great. Let's go pick her up. On the way we need to make a stop. It may sound old-fashioned, but bringing flowers goes a long way. A basic floral arrangement is fine. They do not need to be roses. A small arrangement of seasonal flowers shows her you are sweet because you thought to bring them to her. You want her to be happy and will go out of your way to brighten her day. The other task is to get breath mints. I am an occasional smoker, so I always make sure I go to her door with fresh breath. Even if she is a smoker, I guarantee she would rather be greeted with the smell of mint than that of an ashtray (I know I would).

Always be a gentleman. If you are picking her up at her house, give her the flowers and a compliment. "You look very nice tonight." "I'm glad you wanted to go out with me tonight." "I was looking forward to seeing you." I'm sure if you asked her out, there is something you can compliment her on. If she has a dog, pet it. I don't care if her dog is Cujo, or a hound from hell, if you can pet the dog without getting permanent scars, do it. If she has a cat, don't worry, it probably won't come near you anyway. If it does, pet the cat. Pets are part of the family, so if her pet accepts you, then you are one step closer to her accepting you. Walk *with* her, not in front of her, when you leave the house or are walking to the car. And ALWAYS, I mean ALWAYS open the car door for her. Wait until she gets in the car and then close the door. If she is driving then open her door first and then walk around to the passenger side. The car door is not just a first date action. Get used to it, because it should be a permanent action. It is very important and will be explained more in later chapters.

Labron is sitting nonchalantly at the end of the table. Here is Labron's idea of romance on the first date: after she opens the door, he romantically inquires, "Are you ready to go?" Then, when he walks to the car with her following, hits the unlock button on the remote and points at the passenger side door. He points as if she doesn't know where or how to enter a car, while he walks directly to the driver's side and gets in. What do you suppose this woman is thinking in the first few minutes of this first date? If you pictured her as a light bulb turning off, your right.

You might meet at a coffee shop or a bar for drinks. If

you meet in public, those flowers you brought her have a bonus effect. When you give a woman flowers in public where other women can see, you will get more smiles from women as you are walking to her than you could have imagined. Now they are thinking, "What a great guy. He brought her flowers." She knows that they are looking at you and she is thinking that all the women in the place are checking out the guy she is with. Remember to compliment her and always be a gentleman.

When you both sit down it is very important to sit directly across from her. For the first date, it is important because you are going to be engaging her in a way to gather information. You want be able to view her eyes, mannerisms, habits and overall body language. After this first date, you will rarely be sitting across from her, because you will be sitting *next* to her. Sitting next to her creates intimate space. More about that later. This first date is the opportunity for you to decide if you are sufficiently interested in this woman to invest your time in a second date. Never be afraid to ask her questions. This is another opportunity to use open-ended questions to get information. For example, if you ask "Do you have any brothers or sisters?" She could just say "Yes." If you say instead, "Tell me about your family," she will have a chance to describe some important people in her life. If you ask her how long has she lived in a certain area she could answer, "One year." If you ask her what made her decide to move to this area, you will get the story of where she came from, how long she was there, why she came here and how it turned out. In any situation an open-ended question will get you more information than a yes or no option. People generally like to talk about themselves, so asking the right questions will promote the conversation and you will find out all you want to know about her. And she will feel as though you are interested to learn more about her.

The first date is the time to find out lots of practical information about this potential woman of your dreams. For instance, does she have children? Some men welcome them. How about you? If you are not willing to embrace someone else's children, then you should decide that now, and continue looking for another woman. Dating a single mom is a unique situation because the variable of her children will never change. You have to decide what is right for you. If you feel interacting with her children while dating or living together is going to be uncomfortable, then don't do it. When you date a woman with a child, it is natural for you to be included in the child's life, too. Birthday parties, holidays, school projects...etc. Some guys are willing to accept and enjoy the added family interaction. If you feel this is not for you, then you should be honest about this up front. Just because you do not want to date her further, does not mean you cannot become friends. If you think you are going to just date her anyway knowing you are going to eventually just leave, you would be purposefully hurting her and her children because they will become attached to you emotionally. We all agree this scenario would be just plain WRONG!

While talking to her, pay attention to her body language. One of the ways to connect with a person is mirroring. Mirroring is a rapport-building technique in which one person adopts the physical and verbal behaviors of another.

Mirroring works on a subconscious level, by giving the person the impression that you are just like her or him. However, if she consciously realizes what you're doing she will probably think you're making fun of her, or that you are a jerk. For instance, if you're sitting at a table with someone, notice how they are sitting in their chair. Are they leaning back in a relaxed position? If they are leaning back and you are hunched over the table with your arms stretched half across the table, they might not be feeling very comfortable with you. You might appear pushy and invading their personal space. Are they leaning forward with hands clenched tight on the table? If you are leaning back, slumped in your chair, you might be viewed as aloof and unexcited to be with them. Basically, mirroring is very subtly copying the other person's body language, rate of speech, and style of speaking. Do not, however, copy someone's accent. I can remember when Doug came back from a date and we all thought he was doing a bad James Bond impression. It turned out she was from England and he forgot where he came from.

Hopefully things are going well at this point and you have decided to go from dinner to another destination. She might offer to pay for half the bill. Thank her for the generous offer, but decline and pay the check. Remember when you get to the car, even if she is driving (and especially if she is driving); open the car door for her. Walk her to whichever side of the car she is going into, open the door and close the door after her. Make this a life-long habit. You will hear me mention the car door several times in this book because I can't even count the number of times a woman has said "I am not used to that kind of treatment." It sets you apart from the rest and is part of behavior modification (conditioning).

> **Conditioning:** *learning in which a stimulus initially incapable of evoking a certain response becomes able to do so by repeated pairing with another stimulus that does evoke the response*

She gets in and out her car every day, no big deal. When you repeatedly open the car door for her, she feels the emotional response of caring, kindness and affection from you (and for you). And because you are doing this for her, you are constantly reinforcing these positive emotional feelings. You are evoking an emotional response every time you open the car door for her. Because the act of getting in and out of the car is a common daily occurrence, this is a constant reinforcement. Even if the date is ending and you never want to see her again, be polite and open her door.

If things are going well, it is time to start introducing what I call "intimate space." We all know about personal space. We generally draw a mental boundary around our physical space, and if someone physically gets too close, we become uncomfortable. We all know a person who comes up to talk with you, stands toe to toe, and just starts talking. Unfortunately, only half the time have they had a breath mint after the tuna sandwich they had for lunch.

More importantly, their close physical proximity makes you feel claustrophobic and uncomfortable. Often you will fidget and seek a polite way to back up a bit to a more comfortable distance. Intimate space is sort of the same thing. You have to slowly introduce intimate steps so that she and you are both comfortable in this space. Take the example of when you are going to a movie after dinner. When you are walking to the theater from the car you reach over to hold her hand. Most women would consider this a harmless and sweet gesture. As harmless as it is, you are now slowly and subtlety sharing intimate space. The idea is subtlety. If you kiss her and stick your tongue down her throat when she gets out the car she might respond (you have to judge for yourself) or she will just feel molested. If she feels there was no respect for her intimate space, you have now started a negative response to your intimate space together. If she does not respond well to you holding her hand, it's fine. Perhaps she is not comfortable yet letting you share her space. You can try again later at an appropriate time. In other words, this is a process. If you care enough about her to win her over, Finding Her Sweet Spot could lead to a lifetime of happiness for you both.

At some point the date starts to wind down. In some cases, you realize the date may last until the next morning, in which case the following step is a moot point. The first kiss is an anxiety-filled moment for you and for her. I have known guys who say that they dread that moment because of the pressure; Should I? Shouldn't I? Does she want me to? I don't know. And then it becomes just plain awkward. I have found it is better not to wait until you walk her to her door at the end of a date, but rather to act some time before you take her home. For instance, walking to the car to take her home after dinner is a good time. Only you can decide if the time is right, but look for an opportunity when there is some sense of privacy. She may feel uncomfortable in public because she might be nervous too. Tell her how much you enjoyed your date and spending time with her. I would even suggest making light of the situation. Explain how you feel a first kiss is sometimes awkward and you would like to kiss her. Ask her "Do you mind if I kiss you?" She will probably think it is cute and respectful that you asked. If she says yes, then kiss her, but take it easy-- leave her wanting more. If she wants to continue she will let you know. Follow her lead. You have now taken another step toward intimacy.

By the time you take her home and if all went well you will already have a more comfortable feeling with each other. You have talked, learned a little about each other, shared a meal, shared another activity, held hands and kissed. When you walk her to her door to say goodnight, it will feel natural to give her another kiss and a hug. The hug is important as well. Do not give her a bro hug, a pat on the back hug or a bear hug. I woman likes a hug that feels strong and secure, but soft and vulnerable. I know this is an oxymoron but try to think of what you would say to someone if a hug were words. You are conveying a thought and feelings with your actions. So think about what you would say to her while you give her a hug. This concept should always be in your mind when you hug a friend, relative or anyone you care about. Did you ever hear someone say "He gives great hugs!" The guys are starting to stare at me now, looking confused. While you hug someone and are thinking about the message you want to convey, your body and energy will naturally give just the right pressure and touch. You will be known as the guy who gives great hugs. But be aware if you become the "great hugs" guy, then everyone will want to hug you.

Now that the first date is over, evaluate how the night went, how you feel about her and if you want to continue to invest yourself in this relationship. I don't believe in the three day rule. I have heard so many people talk about how when you get someone's phone number or after a first date, you should wait three days to contact them. That's crazy! Have you ever heard the riddle, "What has a tremendous value even though it's free?" The answer is, your time. Life is short and if you find a woman you are interested in, you should Go For It; leave the games for school kids. If you decided you did not like her, then it's not really an issue. Don't call her at all. If a woman calls you after a first date and you are not interested, just be honest and kind, by letting her know you don't think it would work out for the two of you, you want different things in life etc... But always be honest. If you decided that this woman is awesome, you had a great first date and want to see her again, then call her the next day and tell her. Communication is vital in any relationship, so tell her you had fun, you thought it was a great first date and you would like to see her again. If she feels the same way, she will be very excited and looking forward to seeing you too. A great first date is very exciting. There is an energy and excitement all its own when you first start dating someone new. All your experiences with them are fresh and new. The trick is to keep that newly peaked interest alive and prominent in your relationship. Perhaps it's the excitement of sharing experiences with someone you hope will be the love of your life, or maybe it's the positive energy of knowing you are about to have new life experiences with them.

What do *you* think?

- What's excites you about a new relationship?
- What information would you want to learn about her on your first date?
- What would be a fun first date that you can suggest to a woman you meet?

Step 3 – Reach Out and Touch Someone - Phone Calls and Texts

"Words mean more than what is set down on paper. It takes the human voice to infuse them with deeper meaning."

- Maya Angelou / Author and Poet

After your first date, phone calls and texts are perfect opportunities to establish a positive, playful and sensual rapport. You should be having conversations each evening that deepen and sustain your connection. It is also fun and flirty to exchange a few texts throughout the day. Of course, if you are both more comfortable texting, you could simply have a text-a-thon all day and skip the evening talk. It is important to connect each day in a way that feels meaningful and intimate to you both.

Use these beginning, longer phone conversations to decide if you feel you are compatible physically, emotionally and sexually. When I say physically, I mean that you both like to do the same activities. If I like hiking and rock climbing, and her idea of nature is an indoor plant, you might not being doing that much together. Though there is nothing wrong with couples doing things separately, it is important to also find activities you both like to do together. Maybe you both like sports and the theater. Be open to introducing her to things you love to do, and vice versa. As far as major plans for the future, are you on the same page? Does she want to be married? Have kids? Have a career? Does she like dogs? Does she want to live in the city? The country? Abroad? You want to try and find these things out before you invest too much time and energy into a relationship. She is trying to find out the same information about you, as well she should.

Substantive phone conversations afford you the chance to explore each other's lives more deeply. Don't be afraid to ask the questions you want answered. You can start to learn more about her job, what it was like for her growing up, if she moved here and why, what her goals are for the future and of course her dating habits. Personally, I prefer talking on the phone over text for several reasons. Voice is the most powerful form of communication. It is much more personal than text. Also, emotional conditioning takes place when she hears the tone, frequency and pitch of your voice. She will respond emotionally to the concepts you express, as well as the sound and growing familiarity of your voice. This starts an emotional bond, positive or negative, called voice mapping. As you communicate, she is processing what she does and does not like about you and vice versa. She is comparing that to her past experiences. You are both deciding if the bonding process is positive and gives you good feelings or negative feelings. Of course, if hearing her voice gives you negative feelings, you might not want to invest any more time with her. Our minds are very powerful and process an astronomical amount of information per day. As much as the toughest guy does not want to admit it, men process just as much emotional information as women.

When you start communicating regularly on the phone or through texting, it is time to bestow upon her a special nickname. Bob used to call his girlfriend "Bubba." This is absolutely not what I mean. This is another golden opportunity to use the tool of behavioral modification for a positive response. Especially in the beginning of a relationship when positive emotions run wild and everything is fresh and new, you can install a "feel good" button in her brain. Come up with something appropriate, that you like, and that you can remember. It could be "baby," "buttercup," "lamb chop," "sweet cakes," "lover lips," etc. And of course, she must find it endearing and sweet. When you give her this nickname explain it is for her and for her only because it comes from your heart. She is your (*example:* Cupcake). If you choose well, she will giggle and feel special. Every time you say "Hello Cupcake," she will get a smile on her face and feel warmth in her heart. Using this nickname that nobody else calls her reinforces her intimate bond to you.

Being sexually compatible is very important and often overlooked early in the dating process. Often you will hear (usually from one friend to another) how he or she is not having enough sex with their partner or their partner wants sex more often than they do. You will also hear how one person is more adventuresome than the other, or one person is selfish in bed. All of this has to do with sexual compatibility. Some people might think a discussion like this is premature (no pun intended) but I would like to know some of these details beforehand and so should you. Be cautious. These conversations do require subtlety and respect. Approach the subject in a light-hearted manner, and follow her lead. As I mentioned, most people like to talk about themselves and usually will if given the chance. It will give you an opportunity to share past experiences and be honest about what you desire from a woman. You might find she has a similar libido to yours, or she might be the complete opposite. She might like your ideas and be open to trying new things, or you might find you are interested in trying things her way. But if you can communicate about sex, you will have better sex, and a better chance to make the relationship work. This is an essential component to Finding Her Sweet Spot.

For some people texts feel more natural than speaking. If this is the case, then do what is comfortable for you, but use the same ideas. I like texts for two reasons. 1) It gives you a chance to easily insert dual meanings for flirtatious fun. Because you are not there they perceive what you wrote their way or both ways. 2) You might write something or ask a question you might not ask in person. There is a psychological safety factor to writing something rather than speaking it. Some people are just not comfortable talking about certain subjects face to face but can express themselves without hesitation in writing. So texts can be another valuable communication medium.

Text is awesome because it gives you a chance to easily be a highlight in her day, every day. Depending on how you text you have the option for a response or not. Usually even a single statement will be responded to, or can just send your intended message. Even on your busiest days you can text something like, "Hope you're having a great day!" "Miss you" or "Can't wait to see you later." This takes literally five seconds! Her emotional high from you caring enough to send her a little message within your busy day will have a lasting affect for the rest of her day. And no matter what kind of day she is having, you will get a positive response. When you talk to her later she will say "I got your text today." I don't know how many times I have heard "I was having a great day but it was even better after I got your text." And also, "I was having the worst day ever but after I got your text I was smiling all day." C'mon guys, how cool is it that we can make our women happy, improve their everyday lives, show them we care, and be the romantic hero in literally five seconds? She might not have a chance to respond to your text. That's okay. She might be having a busy day at work. When you do speak to her, she will acknowledge your efforts. Any man with a cell phone not doing this daily needs to reevaluate his priorities and is missing a great opportunity. Utilizing modern technology for a few extra seconds a day is truly a win-win situation for any relationship.

Sexting: *The act of sending explicit message or photographs, primarily between mobile phones. This activity should be engaged in by consenting adults **only**.*

Sexting by definition may sound negative or obscene to some people. But it can be a light-hearted, fun and flirtatious method of foreplay. When you are not with your girlfriend/wife it gives you a chance to tell them you think they are sexy, attractive, and sensual, and that just thinking about them turns you on. Obviously you want to stay at the same speed as your partner. Because if she is sending "I think you're hot" and you are sending explicit scenes from old porn movies where you can almost hear the cheesy background music in your head, this might not achieve the desired goal. You will find her sweet spot more quickly if you "start slow." Be romantic, playful and a little risqué. See where she goes from there. If she is enjoying the game, by all means continue. Just keep appropriate for her pace. It should be fun, not offensive. It is also a great way to keep the relationship spicy. Even after twenty years of marriage, I never heard a woman complain about a text from her husband saying that she was as sexy as the day they met and he was looking forward to their romantic evening. A couple of us were delightfully surprised at how far our women pushed the boundaries of their sexting. You might be surprised too.

An important thought before you have fun sexting: Be sure the phone is not a company phone where other people have access to it. Make certain her cell and yours are personal phones. You might not see the harm or think your boss is not looking at your messages on your company phone, but you don't want to lose your job or risk someone else reading your private messages.

What do *you* think?

- What questions might you be more confident asking over the phone?
- What questions might you feel more comfortable answering through a text?

WILLIAM WRIGHT

Step 4 – The Writing On The Wall - Beginning Dating Rituals

"Real magic in relationships means an absence of judgment of others."

- Wayne Dyer / Author and Motivational Speaker

Sigmund Freud and Herbert Marcuse, two experts on human behavior, theorized that men instinctively spread their affection to increase their odds of finding a mate. Our caveman ancestors evolved to put out "the feelers" to as many prospects as possible to achieve greater reproductive success. The theory is that men were forced into monogamy to adapt to civilization. Think back to a party or gathering you attended. You entered and began your rounds of hellos. While working your way through the crowd looking for the people you know to hang out with, you also took a mental inventory of the women you wanted to meet at some point during the event. "I don't do that at parties," Jeff exclaims. Really? I remember a wedding we all attended for a friend of ours. When Jeff arrived, (late I might add), he walked up to meet us with an enthusiastic smile. "Did you see those adorable bridesmaids and all the hot women at this party?" he asked. Even though he was in a socially awkward position by arriving late, he still took the time to walk around, look and take mental notes of the possible dating matches for himself. It was more of an instinct for him to take the opportunity to walk around the party and determine if there were women he could possibly meet. He knew he would get razzed about being late, but searching for a mate was a stronger instinct than meeting up with his group of friends. The more possibilities you have for success, the better the odds.

We are no longer cavemen, and women will no longer tolerate this behavior. Especially not the one with whom you have chosen to be exclusive. Get in the habit of focusing your affection. We have spent our lives playing the odds. It is time to shower our affections on one woman instead of many. When you are looking for a mate you will have a tendency to give attention to multiple women in the hopes one of them will respond to your attention. In the canine world, males mark their territory and often eligible males will mark a tree so a female can catch his scent. If she likes the scent, the courting rituals can begin. You need to change your mind set now. Sorry, no more peeing on things to leave your mark. It is not always easy and requires more adapting and focusing. Whereas you might have mingled around at a party talking to different women, you will now mingle and flirt more with your girlfriend. If your thought process is, "Well, I already have her," keep in mind you can lose her just as fast. You can still have all the fun and excitement of meeting someone new, just in a different way. In fact, it can be more fun to focus your affection on one person. The familiarity and comfortable feeling with each other can make flirting even more exciting and will build a stronger bond. When you take all the affectionate energy you were sharing and concentrate it on one woman, she will respond to the intensity and channel all of that love and affection right back to you.

Here is a note so crucial I want to post it on a T-shirt, bumper sticker, or maybe the Goodyear Blimp. It's so simple and something that will probably feel natural and comfortable for you, but you don't think of it because it is out of the social norm. In the first part of this book, we established how important it is to sit directly across from your date so you can make eye contact and observe her. That should be the last time you ever sit across from her. After the first date, and forever in your relationship "**You sit next to her!**" Yes, I said "next to her." Jeff does a double take and looks at me like I have two heads. He says, "How weird is that to be at a restaurant, both of you sitting side by side in a booth? What if you are sitting at a table with chairs?" Shaking his head, he adds "That would just feel strange and look weird too!" Let's start with why. This is the next step of sharing intimate space. When you sit next to her you increase physical and emotional intimacy. You can explain to her you want to sit next to her because you want to be closer to her. She will find this romantic and go along with it even if she is not used to the behavior. If she is not used to this behavior, it is even better. You are showing her what a romantic guy you are. She will soon become accustomed to being close to you physically. Of course, this seating arrangement also gives opportunities for hand holding, a touch on her leg, a kiss, or romantically sharing a menu even if you don't have to. Quickly you will find *she* is initiating walking closer to you and being more affectionate. You are creating physical intimacy. Physical intimacy is not just sex. It is an emotional reaction that takes place from any physical touch (holding hands, arm around her shoulder or waist, etc…) When a woman becomes conditioned and comfortable to be close to you physically, she feels connected and safe and she desires to be near you more.

If you are sitting in a place with a square table, choose one of the seats on either side, just not across. When you sit across from someone, you create a space in between. Often this is done when people are together and they are purposely trying to create personal space. For those not in an intimate relationship, it is considered respectful and the socially expected behavior. Because you are trying to build an intimate relationship, you always want to her to have the feeling of comfort from you, and wanting to be close to you. I turn to the guys at the table and ask curiously "Has anyone ever dated a woman who did not prefer you sitting next to her?" Labron answers immediately. "My girlfriend claimed she would rather sit across from me so she could look into my eyes while they we talking. She felt that was more intimate." Labron's girlfriend is more visual than tactile. Labron learned that eye contact made her more comfortable and connected. So he sat across from her, which was the right thing for her.

When you see a couple kissing, walking, holding hands or looking in each other's eyes and smiling, what is your reaction? Do you roll your eyes, simulate gagging noises, smile or just secretly wish you had that same feeling with the one you love? *You* can have that great relationship. You can have the woman of your dreams staring in to your eyes with love and adoration. And the ones rolling their eyes are doing this because they are jealous and frustrated that they do not have the same happiness in their lives. But they can. Sitting next to her is not just for restaurants. It is for any situation in which you can choose where to position yourself. Restaurants give you a consistent opportunity to strengthen this habit. Because we all sit and eat regularly, it will become a recurring trigger or anchor of how you want to be close to her. And she will quickly become very comfortable having you in her personal, intimate space. Sitting next to her, sharing intimate space, regularly creates a comfort level in having you close to her in all situations.

Another lifelong habit to get into is holding her hand or putting your arm around her when you are walking together. The continuous physical contact will reassure her and increase your intimacy level. It will also increase her comfort level with sharing intimate space. Every day habits are what create a foundation for our beliefs. If you regularly touch and show affection to each other, this will quickly become the norm.

When you first start dating someone, make certain that you are being true to yourself. Often we feel like we have to impress a woman to get her to fall in love with us. It is very important that right from the start we share who we really are. If you start out portraying a character you think she will love, the relationship won't work. Eventually your true self will come out. In a long-term relationship, how long can you play a character? Have you ever heard someone say "He or she is like a different person," after they have been together for a while? In many cases this person has been acting like the person they think they should be, until they can't do it anymore. I have seen a woman put on the most convincing performance for about a year. Then it happened. Slowly she returned to her true self, and the difference was significant. From the moment I mentioned that she was acting differently, she resented the fact I was not attracted to the real her, even though we had been together for a year. Of course I would not like to see the person whom I have grown to adore suddenly become a person that I would not have dated in the first place. You should never have to change who you are to impress anybody: a woman, a friend or family. If someone does not like you for the person you are, go meet someone else. If a lot of people don't like you for who you are, perhaps you should take a careful look at yourself and your values. Our lives are enriched by surrounding ourselves with people who are positive, love us, care about us and accept us. Be honest. This way, when you celebrate your fiftieth anniversary with the woman you wooed, she can say "I love him as much now as I did fifty years ago when I married him."

Treat her exactly how you would like to be treated. We all want someone in our lives to care about us, love us, support us, and help us when we need it. Some guys might want a woman who cooks elaborate dinners for them. If she does that for you, how does it make you feel? You feel happy, because she understands you and is willing to go through the effort for you in order to give you joy and pleasure. Ask yourself: do *you* show appreciation for what she does for you? What do *you* do for her that she likes and makes her feel happy and loved? Of course, for everyone it is different. Be aware that every single day of your life your relationship is constantly growing or dying. This is true for every relationship in your life. If you have a good relationship with someone, the bond gets stronger daily. If it is a bad relationship, it will die a little each day.

All relationships require learning how to compromise.

> *Compromise: In arguments, compromise is a concept of finding agreement through a mutual acceptance of terms—often involving variations from an original goal or desire*

This does not mean there is always conflict or that one person always gets their way and the other lives with the consequences. It means no two people are exactly alike. Different people have different views on everything from politics, movies, certain processes to completing a task, styles of furniture, styles of clothes etc.... No two persons will think exactly alike at all times. For example, if the two of you are choosing a movie to go see, you might feel like watching a comedy, but she might prefer a science fiction film. Or you might have a particular genre of movie you like, and she might like something different.

You will have to communicate and learn how to accommodate both of your tastes without one person feeling dominated, always giving in and the other person feeling irritated because of the difficult decision making process. If either party is constantly doing what the other person wants to do, eventually you or she will resent it. This might lead to passive aggressive behaviors, and/or feeling unhappy. You have to establish a style of communication that you are both comfortable with wherein you both feel understood and satisfied with the outcome. It might be seeing the movie she wants to see this week and a promise to see the movie you want next week. But since you are going to the movie she wants tonight, you get to pick the restaurant. Together you can create a win-win situation. Both parties can be happy with the outcome as they develop a stronger bond. The win-win outlook is an effective one to hold from the very start of a relationship. If you both feel small decisions can be made together, and you both benefit from the outcome, it makes it easier to conceptualize that a large disagreement later on could also be resolved with win-win thinking. The mutual win-win scenario is also a fun concept in other ways as well, which I will address later on.

Like everything in life you must focus on what you want and be grateful for what you have. When you are with your new girlfriend or wife, make sure you are focusing on her. Be attentive! Sharing your full attention with her will let her know she is your priority. We often have so many different things going on in our lives, we tend not to focus on what's at hand. People are always trying to multitask. We will be spending time with our significant other while trying to work out some other life issue. In the end, one or the other winds up being ignored. Granted obstacles do arise in life, often at inconvenient times. Some problems do need to be addressed more quickly than others. Don't be afraid to share with her what might be a distracting occurrence for the evening. By sharing life's little distractions with her, you will be amazed at the response. She will feel included in your life. She will also understand if she catches you staring off and nodding while she is telling you that college roommate story you've been waiting to hear. It builds trust between you both. She might even come up with a solution you had not thought of to tackle that obstacle.

This is very good practice for future communication and learning to share your lives together. Every great objective is achieved in steps. One small goal is built upon until you are ready for the next. Then when two small goals have been completed, you can continue your forward progress with greater motivation. The stronger the base, the more it can support. You can build the tallest building in the world as long as the foundation is strong enough. These beginning trials will help build the trust, love and respect for a solid future together.

She has obstacles in life just like you do. Being attentive to what's going on in her world as well as your own is essential. You should check in with her every day and know about her ups and downs. This will make you truly a part of her life and will build intimacy. Make sure to ask about her day. Be encouraging and positive. Be a good listener, a sounding board for those not so great days we all have. Building the trust and comfort level to share a negative experience takes time. For instance, if you get a promotion at work, you're running up and down the halls, and pumping your fists to your sides, while thrusting your pelvis forward. You yell "Yes, yes, yes!" and then you tell "everyone" and go out to celebrate your success. If, on the other hand, you get passed up for a promotion at work, you might call only a couple of people closest to you to share your disappointment quietly. You want her to feel as though you are a person she can share her negative life events with as well as the positive. We share our learning experiences (only negative people call them failures) with our closest friends because we know they will not judge us. They will share our disappointment, understand us and comfort us.

Become her best friend. She will always have a best girlfriend to share certain things which men may never understand, but we all have a best friend. It is the person we will call and tell the most embarrassing, outrageous, stupid, drunken thing we did last night, knowing he/she will not hold it against us and will keep our secret. (Chances are you will get drunk one night and tell everyone anyway). You want to be that "Best Friend" to her. The first person she wants to call, the person she trusts most, celebrates with, cries with, and is willing to be silly with. Because she knows you will not judge her, she regards you with trust, not fear. Becoming her best friend connects you on multiple emotional levels. But remember you have to earn it! Sounds heavy right? Being this best friend to her makes you an especially important person in her life. Make sure you don't abuse the best friend privilege, but rather, embrace it. Your goal is to become best friends for life. The more emotional levels on which you can connect with her, the stronger your emotional bond will become.

When you are out together, Do Not Look At Another Woman! Your focus should be totally on her. Women are very observant in a way that men cannot even fathom. They will notice things you or I would fail to see, even if someone left a sticky note on your forehead. And if you think they don't see you looking over a menu, or out the glass window or the obvious whiplash head turn you made to look at another woman, you are sadly mistaken. Bob asks, "How can I not look? I'm not dead!" He also claims he is very discreet when he looks, "She never knows." Bob is not dead, except from the neck up. If you can't control your eyes, be the horse's ass you are and put on blinders. Do whatever it takes to train and control yourself. When a woman catches you looking at another woman, she will not merely think you are being disrespectful. She is going to feel hurt, and will question your loyalty. She will wonder if you are committed to her or looking for someone better. When she starts to doubt your sincerity in the relationship, she is going to look for someone more stable. You want her to grow to love you, not distrust you. Here is a great habit to get into: Each time you see a woman that catches your eye, turn and give your girlfriend or wife a sweet kiss. She will find this kiss out of nowhere to be very romantic and sweet, and it will remind you both of why you want to be together.

When you are out with other people socially, Do Not Touch Another woman! When I say that, I don't mean a hand shake, a hug hello, or the friendly kiss on the cheek good friends might share. I am talking about putting your arm around a female friend and then leaving it there, or a hug that lasts beyond its expiration date. NEVER walk holding another woman's hand in front of your girlfriend or wife (unless it's your daughter). And most of all, No Intimate Touching of Another Woman, friend or not, in front of your girlfriend or wife. Of course, you shouldn't be doing that when she is not around either. I don't care if your woman says, "Oh, don't worry." "I'm not jealous." Or "It's innocent." Do not buy into this. Anytime your girlfriend sees you touch another woman intimately, you psychologically break your bond with her. The more she sees this, the more the intimate separation between you will build. If intimacy is shared among many people, it's not intimate anymore. Don't touch another woman's hair, neck, back, front, legs, feet, toes or face. I think I covered all the body parts. As I've said before, women notice everything. Women notice what other women are doing, what men are doing, and what the people down the street that they can't even see are doing. In other words, they are observant. For the guys who claim that an innocent touch is nothing, imagine your girlfriend or wife giving her super good-looking guy friend an innocent full body massage. This is a close comparison with what she is thinking and feeling. So before you nonchalantly give that personal touch to someone else, think twice and go give your girlfriend or wife a big hug and kiss. Remember, every action you take brings you closer together or further apart.

Get in the habit of kissing when you come and go. Obviously there is an emotional response when you kiss someone. When you kiss someone at different times and under different circumstances you get a different response. The kiss, along with the right verbal communication, stimulates a bigger response. We teach children to use their words when they want something, rather than whining or pointing. Adults must also use their voice. When you kiss her goodbye before leaving, say "I love you," or "I will miss you today." This assures her that you care about her and would rather be spending time with her. When you see her after a long day, give her a kiss, and say "I missed you," or "I Couldn't wait to see you." She will know you were thinking about her when she wasn't around and that you love her. When you do this regularly you are creating a habit, and she will look forward to kissing you. It will quickly get to the point that, if you don't kiss her, she will think something is wrong. You are creating continued intimacy that will grow quickly. She will soon initiate the intimacy at all levels, because it will become a behavioral pattern. She will return ten-fold the emotional effort you put in to the relationship.

When you are in relationship, it is inevitable that you will talk a lot. From the start, search for topics that you have a common interest in such as authors, sports, history, politics, science, current events, religion, art, music, etc. It is important to have some sort of intellectual connection also. Stimulating conversation, and game play such as board games and card games, creates another form of bonding. Connecting on an intellectual level which is non-emotional is important too. The exchange of thoughts and ideas are what challenges our brain. Most people crave topical discussions of possibilities, truths and new discoveries in areas we find interesting. Connecting on as many levels as possible is to your advantage and builds a stronger bond.

Be spontaneous. A great way to appeal to a woman's emotional charge is to do something unexpected. Be a little outrageous or a lot, whatever suits your personality. I remember being in a diner where they have the music boxes at the tables. When a song came on that we both liked, I could tell that she had that romantic look in her eyes. So I slid out of the booth and put my hand out to take hers. She stared at me with a puzzled look, and we then danced in the middle of the restaurant. At some point, I looked at her face and she was just beaming with affection. People watched with disbelief. Many women watched with admiration and jealousy. When we sat down after our dinner show, she said, "I can't believe we just did that. It felt like I was in the spotlight at Prom." She was overwhelmed and elated by a simple gesture that I thought was something fun and unusual to do.

Simple romantic gestures cost you nothing, but will make her feel like a fairytale princess. If you make her feel like a fairytale princess, then you are the fairytale prince. I have danced with a woman in restaurant, a park, on the hood of my car on the I-95, in a supermarket and in a Reggae dance contest in front of hundreds of people. (Side note about the dance contest--we did not even come close to winning or looking professional in any way shape or form. It was just fun and we had a great time.) Obviously I am big on the dancing. You have to find the spontaneous and outrageous things that your girlfriend would have fun doing. Small, inexpensive gifts, at unexpected times, are very spontaneous. I am not saying you should buy a woman's affection. Your unexpected gifts should be small tokens that she will know required some thought. Perhaps she has a favorite candy bar, author, musician or flavor of coffee. Give her something simple that shows you pay attention to what she likes.

Music can be a very powerful emotional cue. Music is all around us. On television, every commercial has music and a tag line which we are conditioned to remember after hearing it over and over. Have you ever noticed when you are walking through a mall, there is music? This is designed to put you in the mood to shop and make purchases. Most restaurants play music as well. In the convenience store, supermarket, drugstore, salon, and just about every retail location, you will hear music playing in the background. There is a reason they play music and specific types of music in different locations.

Music can cue a wide range of emotions such as happiness, sadness, love, hate, calm, rage and everything in between. The largest part of the brain is the cerebral cortex, which has two sides, the left and right brain. The right side of your brain processes information in an intuitive, creative, and imaging manner. The left side of your brain is involved with analytical thinking, such as verbal or mathematical matters. The Corpus Callosum connects the left and right brain hemispheres and facilitates communication between the two sides. Scientists have proven that music can affect your mood and emotions because it allows your left and right brains to communicate. Music therapy is accomplished by combining specific music with exact speech to reach the desired outcome. We have all listened to a song that made us feel so energized and powerful that we couldn't help moving our hands to simulate drumming or jamming on the guitar. Heavy metal music often has this effect on me. Imagine the song "Take me out to the ball game." Perhaps you are getting an image in your head of a baseball field with green grass, and stands full of people swaying and singing. Maybe you can even smell the hotdogs, popcorn and beer.

Have you ever heard a powerful singer belting out a love ballad? As the emotion, power and pitch in their voice builds to a climax, people will start to cry as they are overwhelmed with emotion. Understanding these musical cues and how they affect emotions in your relationship is very important, particularly in two different areas. You have your everyday, feel good, feel connected listening music and your intimate space, bedroom music which we will talk about in a later chapter. Actively search for the music you both like, that is positive, energetic and bonding for you both. Whether it is an individual artist or genre, in the future as you hear these songs it will cue a positive memory and an emotional feeling of happiness and well-being.

Let's say you're driving together to a friend's house on a Sunday afternoon. The sky is blue and the sun is shining. It's warm outside, but not too warm. A slight breeze is blowing, which feels very refreshing. While driving in the car a song comes on the radio and you look at each other and say "Oh, I love this song" so you crank it up a little louder. As you're listening you both start bopping your heads and singing the words to the song. At some point you look at each other and laugh because you know you both look silly, but "Who cares?" You're having fun. It's a beautiful day for a car ride. You're feeling good, singing, and sharing it with someone you care about. Years from now that song will come on the radio and she will get a smile from the happy memory.

Creating a positive memory through music is very powerful. Be careful though, because this goes both ways. You can create a very powerful negative memory as well in which every time she hears a song, artist or type of music she feels angry and upset with you. If you do suspect a negative memory was created, try to replace that memory with a positive memory.

What do *you* think?

- Has being overly physically affectionate with other women landed you in the doghouse in the past?
- How do you typically resolve conflict with your significant other?
- What's the benefit for you to create intimate physical space with your girlfriend/wife?

WILLIAM WRIGHT

Step 5 – The Inquisition - Meeting Her Friends and Family

"Sometimes your truest family started out simply as friends."

- William Wright / Author

At some point you will be called to face "The Inquisition." You will have to meet her friends and family. If you are expecting to be questioned, dissected and judged, you are correct. Her friends want to see how you rate compared to previous boyfriends, and how you will fit into their group. Her mom will be interested in how you treat her, and if you are good for the long term. Her father will be focused on whether you are good enough for his little girl. Sure, no pressure! Some men feel nervous about meeting their girlfriend's relatives and friends. They fear that if they don't like and accept him, he will lose the girl. This is not necessarily true. Nevertheless, you *do* want to try to make a favorable impression upon the people to whom she is closest. It will make future social gatherings easier and more comfortable if you all get along. If she does value the opinions of her friends and family, you definitely want to put your best efforts forward to blend in with them. Remember your friends and family will be doing the same with her, because they care about you.

Be prepared to be inundated with a barrage of questions ranging from your job, to any history of mental illness in your family (usually asked by the craziest member of her family). Jeff tells us the story of how he accidentally got ambushed. Jeff's coworker approached him about meeting a single woman his wife knows. They were going to a holiday barbeque at another person's house and wanted Jeff to come and meet her. After hearing the description of this girl, he happily agreed. Before the barbeque, Jeff went home to get ready. He showered, put on his cologne, and dressed one step up from what one would wear to a barbeque. He was determined to make a good impression because he didn't know who was going to be at the house, and he might have some competition. On the way, he stopped to pick up a dessert item to bring. This is always a polite thing to do when you go to someone's house. When he arrived, he gave the dessert to the hostess, walked in, and was greeted by the other guests. About half way through the introductions he started to realize all these people were related: brothers, sisters, mother, cousins, etc....This was no ordinary barbeque--this was a family picnic, and the girl was her sister. Typically, a first date and meeting the entire family are two separate events. But, he was already there, and had already met everyone, so the date was on. He had nothing to lose. As it turned out, by being prepared for meeting the woman, he ended up impressing her whole family. The family was as crazy as the day is long. He said it was more like a wild daytime talk show than a barbeque. But, he liked the girl and decided to see her again. He figured at least he already met the family, so from then on it would be smooth sailing.

When you meet her friends, don't be nervous. The questions they are going to ask you are the same as if you were to meet any new group of people. The good part is you all have something in common; you all like the woman who brought you. Think of it from a positive point of view. It gives you the opportunity to expand your social network of friends, and perhaps you might meet someone you have a lot in common with and create a new friendship. By meeting her friends, you also get to learn about her. Friends are always glad to share stories with the new person (whether they like it or not). And they will tell you stories about her she wouldn't normally tell you for a while. You will quickly learn new things about her and the people she enjoys hanging out with. People love to talk about themselves and their group, so keep those open-ended questions coming and you will gain a lot of information about them as well. Also, it gives you a chance to assess her group of friends. Are you going to enjoy socializing with them if you date her regularly? When you start dating someone, you also expand the social group you will be spending time with.

When meeting her family, don't be nervous. (Unless her aunt who is a nurse comes over wearing a rubber glove and holding a specimen cup. Don't worry this only happened to me once). When you meet her family, just treat them as if they were your own family. However, you definitely want to treat them better than Labron treats his own family. Labron's idea of a family gathering is finding the food, and then finding a couch to nap on. Keep in mind as you meet these people that they could potentially end up being your family. So, learn to interact and blend in with them. Learn who they are and what roles they play in the family circle. To fit in with her family, instantly pretend you are already a member of the family. Her mom will start treating you like she would her son, so be the good son. When her mom sees you are willing to take on the role of boyfriend and possible husband for her daughter, she will accept you in the "possible son-in-law" role. You might be asked to do more than her real children would do, but that's okay. Her acceptance will reassure her daughter that she is making the right decision to be with you. In fact, if her mom accepts you, she will encourage her to continue to stay with you, and question if she is treating you well.

Always interact with her mom respectfully. You should refer to her as Mrs. X, and then if her mom seems like a pretty easy-going person, and appears to be taken with you, you can increase your status in the family unit by calling her "Mom." Make sure to ask her permission first, "Do you mind if I call you Mom?" It shows you are respectful for asking first, and she will feel that you care about her. If she is agreeable, and they usually are if you ask sweetly, you will set another positive anchor in your relationship with your girlfriend and her family. This does not usually work the same way with her father, although in some cases it might. Do what you feel is right for you. The relationship between two men differs somewhat, especially with the father who feels that he is the protector of the family. Generally the protector will take longer to feel comfortable that his baby girl is safe with you. He will remain suspicious longer, but just like building any other relationship, your honesty, respect and positive actions will eventually win him over.

If she is close with her family, and you alienate her family, you will put a strain on your relationship that will grow over time. As much as possible, participate in family events like weekly dinners and holidays. This will help you bond with the family. The more involved you are with her family, the easier it will be for her to imagine a future with you. And if your family doesn't live nearby, this is also an opportunity to enjoy that family closeness you might be missing. Look at this from a positive perspective; you have the chance to have a whole other family to bond with and another social group to enjoy life's meaningful events with.

On several occasions, I have become very close with the parents of a girl I was dating. Sometimes it was her mom, her dad or both. I currently have many friends who I consider "family" that I speak to on a regular basis. I met many of these people originally through a woman I was dating. I may no longer be close to the woman I was dating, but I formed such a tight bond with her parents and other family members, we chose to continue our relationship regardless. Some people might consider this strange or wrong, but if you like someone and have formed an authentic bond, then regardless of how you met why not include them in your life and continue to enjoy their company as individuals.

I can recall a particular situation with a woman (let's call her Mary) I dated for a long time. I had become close with her father (Matthew), and we would often hang out without her as friends. I believe he felt I was treating his daughter very well, and started to think of me as his future son-in-law. For years we built this bond separately from larger family gatherings. At some point, Mary and I broke up. I continued to talk to her dad regularly. Shortly after, I started dating someone new. As a result, Matthew and I had to have the conversation that I had moved on to another woman. We both wished to continue an active friendship. He told me as much as he would have liked to have seen things work out between me and his daughter, he understood. Soon Matthew and his wife were spending time with me *and* my new girlfriend. When Mary found out, she was furious. She told her parents that if they did not stop talking to me, she would disown them. This was quite the dilemma for them. They felt she was being childish; we had built a very strong bond and they were confused. I understood Mary's strong feelings about this, so I discussed the situation with her mom and dad, and we all agreed it would be better for us not to hang out for a while. They still wanted to keep in touch, but not go out together. Eventually Mary and I resumed an amiable and platonic friendship. At that point, she was accepting of me and her parents hanging out together because she understood how close we had become. This is an unusual situation. But you just never know what types of emotional bonds and friendships you will encounter in your life. Today, I still talk to her parents and see them when I am in town. It is a relationship I will value for many years to come.

What do *you* think?

- Have you been comfortable with your girlfriend/wife's family in the past?
- Do you enjoy socializing with your significant other's friends?
- What's the benefit for you to get to know your woman's social circle better?

WILLIAM WRIGHT

Step 6 – Woo Hoo! - Sex For The First Time

"The greater our knowledge increases, the more our ignorance unfolds."

- John F. Kennedy / 35th President of the United States

Now we are getting to the good stuff. Having sex the first time with someone new has an excitement all its own. It's difficult to describe this heightened sense of emotional and physical anticipation. It is a little like test driving a new, ultrafast sports car. You have driven a car before, but every car performs differently. So the anticipation of the possible speed and handling makes your blood pump faster. For those pure adrenaline junkies out there, it's like the first five seconds after you jump out of a plane while skydiving. The blood rushes to your head, your brain knows there is no turning back, you have conquered your fear, and you just enjoy the incredible rush. You anticipate the experience. The excitement builds until you can hardly contain yourself. The act itself is pure euphoria.

For the guys out there who don't know this, women enjoy the heightened pleasure of *I-want-to-tear your-clothes-off-because-I-can't-wait-to-get-to-your-naked-body* type of sex too. In fact, women crave primal sex just as much as men do. But there are different physical and emotional triggers to get men and women to that same stage.

Before this point, you should have had conversations about what you both like sexually. For some people these conversations are embarrassing or uncomfortable to have. They serve a dual purpose: 1) To find out if you are sexually compatible. That is not to say you or she is not willing to try something the other likes, but there are definite differences in sexual styles and preferences. You might be surprised at your comfort with trying new things because of how you feel about the woman you're with. I think all men have engaged in something we never thought we would ever do, because she really liked it. 2) To find out what she likes so you can fully please her. Satisfying her sexually goes a long way to creating a deeper emotional bond. We are all sexual creatures and you may find that satisfying her sexually may compensate for another area where your bond is growing more slowly. Communicating openly about a sensitive subject helps us to improve communication on other levels too. If we can talk about sex so openly, we can talk about anything easily.

Condoms! First time, Every time. No ifs, ands, or buts. Unless you would choose to be a parent right now, use a condom. If you would not choose to contract a sexually transmitted disease, HIV or something else antibiotics can't cure, use a condom. I always recommend both parties getting medically tested. If a woman tells me she does not like condoms and does not want me to use one, I would leave! I would rather find another woman who cares more about her life and mine. My first priority is keeping me and my penis safe. I hope it is for you too.

The number one rule for the first time having sex with a woman and to ensure she wants more and more and more is…. It's All About Her! I repeat, It's All About Her! Men, let's be honest, we can get excited by a strong wind or sometimes just by breathing. Men have a more physical response to sex than women do. Most men can be instantly aroused by almost anything they see, touch, taste, smell, hear or imagine. A woman's sexual arousal works differently; it is more emotional and physical. Depending on the man, you can obtain an erection and have an orgasm anywhere between one and eight times in a night. This depends on age, testosterone levels and fitness. But no matter the circumstances, unfortunately we can only have one single orgasm at a time. Women, on the other hand, can have multiple orgasms every time they have sex or are aroused (lucky them).

If it is available to you, the second rule is Use The Music. We discussed earlier some of the emotional effects of music. Whether the mood is for Barry White, Barry Manilow, Metallica, Sinatra, Usher, Lady GaGa, Flo Rida, Eminem or Alvin and The Chipmunks (which might be slightly creepy but I'm not judging), use it. Music can be an emotional trigger for romantic, playful, wild, deeply emotional or whatever kind of sex you want to have. Set the tone. Playing that same style of music will later initiate an emotional and physical response, so you want to make it a positive one. Even a person with little interest in music who has the worst rhythm on the planet will eventually start to move and sway with the right music. From a physical perspective, it can help to keep you both in the same mood and rhythm at the same time. The more the two of you are in sync, physically and emotionally, the better the sex will be.

The third rule is that anything worth doing is worth doing right. In general this means there are steps we have to take to prepare for anything we are doing. And if we take the time and prepare properly, the outcome will be successful. Have you ever heard this saying, referring to a woman "You have to preheat the oven before you can cook?" It is true!

Foreplay:

1: erotic stimulation preceding sexual intercourse,

2: action or behavior that precedes an event.

Guys, you have heard about this. Most of you know what it is, but, according to statistics, less than half of you do it. If you want to create a strong sexual bond with a woman you care about, and please her more often sexually, learn about foreplay. It is part of the sexual experience. Enjoy it. Have fun with it. The more you do it, the more she will enjoy your physical relationship. It will differentiate you from her past lovers, and she will want to have more and more satisfying sex with you in the future. If you are not sure what foreplay is, take the time to learn. In this wonderful computer age, it is easy to learn and I encourage you to research it. Later on I will have other topics I will encourage you to research and learn about on the Internet as well, to help you understand her better.

Never rush. Not to say an occasional quickie can't be hot and sexy, but it should not be the norm. Take your time. As comedian Robin Williams once joked about sex "Pack a lunch and stay for the day." Before intercourse ever takes place, you should have explored every inch of her body front and back, head to toe. Take the time to learn about her body, what she responds to and what she doesn't. She will clue you in physically and verbally as you are going along. Pay attention to all the details, because some women might get turned on when you kiss a peculiar spot on her leg just above the back of her left knee, and you should learn this. I like to call these the "external G spots." These physically arousing spots on her body will be of great advantage and pleasure for you both. I once dated a woman who would get extremely sexually excited when I rubbed her stomach. Who would have thought? But by paying attention and talking to her about it, I learned that every time I stood behind her and started rubbing her stomach she would get so excited she would almost have an orgasm. At that point, all she wanted to do was find the nearest convenient place to have sex. And I learned that when I was in the mood I knew just how to let her know. It was also fun to tease her in public because nobody would think anything odd about me having my arms around her, but she would be getting all worked up. By the time we would get home later, the oven was well heated up. Do you think she told me about this when we first started dating? No, she didn't. In fact I don't think she realized it before. It was something we both realized while talking one day. For some reason, that particular action, from when we first started having sex, became an erotic trigger for her. I do know that trigger would not have been discovered or reinforced if I had not considered foreplay an exciting and fun part of our sexual relationship.

While in bed, ask her what she likes. It amazes me how some people feel awkward about talking during sex. I'm not talking about her looking up to ask "Is the garage door open?" If she does that, there is a whole other problem. You are engaging in something enjoyable and meaningful. You can talk and share. Ask her if there is something particular she finds pleasurable. Maybe there is something particular she likes to do. Don't forget a good woman wants you to be happy too, and may want to do things to please you. Or, what she might like doing is for *your* pleasure. Let her guide you to what she is comfortable with. You want her to feel comfortable and safe being with you. If she feels comfortable and safe with you sexually, as time goes on, she will be open to trying more adventurous escapades that she or you always wanted to try.

For the benefit of Javier sitting next to me, I point out that a clitoris is not an exotic plant. At that moment Roxanne our waitress walks by, and, overhearing my comment to Javier, responds with a resounding "Amen," followed by a smile and playful wink. Javier is now looking at me funny, kind of sarcastically, but still confused.

I have **never** heard a man say "That's okay, I don't really want oral sex." That's because the penis has the most sensory nerve endings on your body, which means it feels *really good* when stimulated. The clitoris is the female equivalent to the penis. Her clitoris has more sensory nerve endings then your penis. Most vaginal orgasms are achieved not by penetrating the vagina, but in combination with clitoral stimulation from intercourse. If you want to give her great orgasms and multiple orgasms you need to start including her clitoris. You can stimulate her clitoris as foreplay or to full orgasm by hand or oral sex. But remember her clitoris is more sensitive than your penis so communicate with her about pressure and the style that feels good for her. Some men prefer less pubic hair on a woman and would give her clitoris more attention if it were trimmed. In this case, just explain to her how you feel and let her know you care enough to make it worth her while to trim or shave. Chances are if you ask her, she will do it, knowing she will turn you on even more.

I am far from a Type A personality, but I do believe that if I am going to do something I want to do it the right way. I know this is going to sound unconventional, but researching on the Internet or the library about how a woman's body works would absolutely be to your advantage. Men are pretty basic and we have been grabbing ourselves since we first realized we had a penis. Have you ever heard a lesbian say that sex is great with her partner because nobody knows a woman's body better than another woman? It's because women have been refining their masturbation skills since they discovered how their vaginas work. If you own it, you are familiar with it. I believe most men would be amazed by how the female body works and where all the parts are located. When I say "research," I am not talking about porn. I am talking about her anatomical physical body. If you have a better understanding of how the female body works, you will have the knowledge of how you can bring her the most pleasure.

For some people, the moments after sex for the first time can be a little awkward. Everyone has their own expectations and experiences. That does not mean if there is a three second silence you jump up and head for the shower. Get in the habit of snuggling after sex. For a woman, the emotional response lasts beyond the physical act. Start getting in the habit of bonding emotionally after sex. For a woman, the concert might be over but there is still an after party. Even if it is understood you are not going to stay the night, stay for the after party. Get used to being comfortable in a shared emotional and vulnerable environment. It doesn't get more intimate than this. The shared bond that is created lying in each other's arms after sex is very, very strong. If she feels that you are staying in bed to bond with her it reinforces her feeling that you will stay around at other emotional times for support. She will start to trust you more and feel supported by you. The more she feels comfortable with you being around during an emotional or vulnerable situation, the stronger her trust and love will grow.

The day after you have shared very intimate time together you must be aware of her emotional state. As men, we are happy, we just had sex, we are happy we met this wonderful woman and oh, a football game is on TV.

Stay focused. Make sure to reinforce the positive feelings she is having. If you don't see her the next day, make certain to call. Text is not good enough here. Voice recognition is important. It is your voice from the night before, the voice that made her feel so happy and satisfied. The call is to reassure her that her feelings about you are correct, that you are caring and communicative, and that she made the right decision to sleep with you. This also gives you the chance to discuss the highlights of the night before and to let her know you felt the same way she did. Generally, for women, the decision to have sex with someone is more than just who is available. You want them to feel like they made a wise choice not only to sleep with you, but to continue having a relationship. If you reassure her, she is going to want to know when she is going to see you again.

Nothing is quite as sensitive as a male libido. Every man wants to be spectacular in bed and fully satisfy his woman. The male libido can be affected by emotional and physical issues. Sometimes these symptoms are related. Dr. Mehmet Oz, the world renowned physician whom I highly respect, practices both traditional and alternative medicine. He believes, as I do, that "not everything is cured with a pill." He recommends several natural foods to boost the libido. He also recommends some natural remedies that in some cases can help men with Erectile Dysfunction (Natural Viagra or Libido Enhancers). All of this information and more is sourced in his books and on his website.

All Natural Libido Boosters

Asparagus – Contains folates necessary for histamine production. Histamine is released during orgasms.

Pumpkin Seeds – High Zinc content. It blocks enzymes that convert Testosterone to estrogen.

Halibut – High in Magnesium. Helps to increase Testosterone levels.

Ginger – Dilates blood vessels to increase blood flow. Can help increase blood flow to the genitals.

Bananas – Contain Bromolain which aids in triggering greater production of testosterone.

Garlic – A major source of Allicin, which helps gets blood circulation to the genitals.

Oysters – Packed with Zinc. They improve sperm and testosterone production as well as increase dopamine, which causes feelings of pleasure.

Dark Chocolate – Delivers a blast of flavonoids, which increases blood flow to the genitals, as well as phenyethylamine, which causes feelings of love.

All Natural Libido Enhancers (Natural Viagra)

Some benefits of the following natural remedies can be; an increase sexual function, immune health, fatigue and stress relief.

- Asian Ginseng
- Rhodiola
- Maca
- Ashwagaanda Tea

Though these are all natural remedies, I encourage you research any products before use. And consult a physician about any interactions or health risks with medications you might be taking. Remember, safety first.

What do *you* think?

- Have you ever decided it was okay not to use a condom?
- How lucky did it turn out for you? (Notice I said lucky.)
- Would women describe you as an exciting and generous lover, or are you selfish and uninspiring in bed?

WILLIAM WRIGHT

Step 7 – Practice Makes Perfect – Spending Time Together

"People may hear your words, but they feel your attitude."

- John C. Maxwell / Author and Speaker

Now that you have met this great woman, were introduced to her friends and family and are hopefully growing a spectacular sexual relationship, what is next? As this relationship grows, you will be spending ever increasing amounts of time together. If you find that every time you see her you are learning something new about her which brings you closer together, your excitement for the relationship will continue to grow. In a parallel manner, her feelings about your budding relationship are starting to blossom as well. Doug says, "I always enjoy the excitement of a new relationship. The Ether is still strong" and "so am I." Doug is referring to a sales term. *Ether* is what they call it when you are feeling very excited about purchasing an item. You have that elated feeling about something new, but have not yet evaluated the full spectrum of the purchase. Is it the right one for me? Is there a large amount of maintenance required for this item? Can I afford the payments? Is it practical? Buyers don't start thinking about the secondary, long term consequences until the "Ether" wears off. The second part of Doug's comment refers to his initial commitment to the relationship. Doug is implying that with past women he has over time grown a little lazy and apathetic about putting forth the effort and time required to build and keep a strong relationship. This is why he has a history of relationships that dwindle in intensity after a short while. Eventually, one or both decide to move on to something new.

A strong relationship is like anything else worthwhile in life. It takes time, energy and commitment. Like all of our goals in life, you have to have a plan, work hard and make the commitment to yourself to do whatever it takes to achieve it. Professional athletes train an incredible number of hours for just one contest. All that training is not just utilized in one tournament, but for many. Their training is a continual building of their minds, muscles, skills and stamina for many events to come. If you look at a bodybuilder, you only see his muscular and sculpted physique. Have you ever considered the commitment required to train physical bodies to achieve that level of fitness? It requires a lifestyle that most of us could not mentally or physically endure: the hours spent at the gym, the restricted diet, physical pain of injuries, and the mental fatigue of pushing themselves beyond their expected limits. Most athletes must also maintain a full time job to pay their bills while training and focusing to win the contest they are entered in. It's not as simple as is looks. You see the result of his or her hard work, not the process it took to get there. It is the same for anyone who is at the top of their field. The best computer programmers in the world, people who have created the incredible video games you play, and the computers that run the defense systems that protect our country have that same passion and commitment. They have to learn what it takes to create these systems and delve deeply into their minds for their creative solutions. They have trained their minds to think in ways you or I would not ever imagine. It requires commitment to achieve your goals.

For those people who have a goal, the process and the commitment is everything. If your goal is to build a long-lasting and loving relationship with the woman you desire, you have to make the commitment to do what it takes to achieve it and keep it growing. When I think of a long term goal of a relationship with a woman, I think of a happy, exciting, loving and respectful relationship for life. We are always growing stronger and sharing experiences together. If you have ever looked at your birth certificate, you will see it has a birth date, but not an expiration date. From this I can conclude that the only one who is sure when I am going to expire is my Maker. I could be on this earth for a very short time or a very long time. Either way, I want to make the most of every day and share it with someone I love and care about. Understand that commitment does not necessarily have to be work. You can commit to having fun. You can commit to taking vacations, taking walks in the park, trying a new type of food once a month, or always having fun with your girlfriend or wife. You are merely deciding to take actions in the future to achieve your goal.

Commitment: an agreement or pledge to do something in the future.

Now that you are at the point when you are spending more time together, it is a great opportunity to experiment. At some point in the relationship you will have an occasion to stay overnight at her home or yours. This is the time to start building comfortable routines in the evening and the next morning. We all have our own unique routines in life. At night, do you brush your teeth before you change for bed or after? Do you prefer the temperature cooler or warmer when you sleep? Do you keep a glass of water next to the bed? Do you sleep on the left side or the right side of the bed? You have your routines and she has hers. Most times two people can share space without interrupting each other's daily rituals. Mornings can be a little more challenging when two people work and have to be out of the house on time. In the morning, what time do you wake up? What time does she wake up? Who showers first? What time do you each have to leave the house? When you start to stay overnight you will begin to learn to share a space and maybe adopt new habits to accommodate each other.

Make certain she feels comfortable in your home. Keep it clean and tidy. It shows her you are independent and mature. If you are constantly telling people who come through your front door, "Sorry about the mess, it's my bachelor pad," then it's time to clean up! Remember, you only have one chance to make a first impression. It doesn't matter if you live in a studio apartment, or a penthouse suite, your environment shouldn't represent you as lazy or a slob. If she comes to your house and has to step over dirty laundry, or sees dirty dishes all over the coffee table and kitchen counters, she will think, "I *really* don't want to clean up after him." Most women aren't looking to move in with someone for whom they have to be a maid. If she knows you will leave a big mess all over the house and not care, she will automatically consider it a negative idea. It also creates the image that you are not mature or responsible. If you can't even pick up your dirty underwear, or clean off the table, how are you going to handle guests in the house, or eventually, children? When you bring her to your home it should look tidy and neat. It shows you care about your self-image and your level of maturity. I am not saying it should be hospital disinfected and spotless at all times. But nobody wants to hang out at someone's dirty, smelly house. If she were to walk into your disastrous bachelor pad and not be affected by chaos, you should be concerned. If she has the same home décor values that you have, you can only imagine the house with both of your messes mixed together (a hazardous materials sign may be needed).

The same cleanliness guideline applies to your car. Some people do have a career that requires spending much of their time traveling in the car. Plus, we all know how easy it is to accumulate junk in the back seat area. Most women don't want to have to kick your papers and trash to the side just to get in your car. Not to mention the smell from old stale food and drink cups. Consider this, how many of you guys would like to have your girlfriend or wife, who is feeling very romantic and adventurous, ask you to go to the back seat of your car for some fun? Or maybe it was your idea? All the guys at the table are now starting to grin. Do you think if she looked back there and saw piles of garbage and old food she would still want to go back there? The answer is no. You would just be sitting there sad and disappointed; as she told you she changed her mind. So clean it up, make it inviting, and make it look like you care enough to do it for yourself. My other personal tip is to always keep a blanket in the car. It might get chilly, or you might come across a romantic to spot to sit outside, and you will be prepared with a blanket to sit on. Be prepared for romantic opportunities.

If the overnight visits go well, you will go on to weekend stays. Spending weekends at her or your home is an awesome way of getting used to sharing space. When you are going to stay for the weekend, you usually have a little more gear, but not too much. You can experience what it is like when both of your daily rituals are intertwined. You get to experience sharing intimate space, living space and personal space. It really is a quick peek to see what it's like living together. This should be an absolute necessity before ever considering moving in together. As much as you might fall in love quickly and feel she is Mrs. Right, always take the time to experiment with smaller scenarios. When you spend a weekend with your girlfriend, you should not be putting on a show. Do what you would normally do or not do. It is a learning experience for you and her. Behavior is different when you spend a short or long time period with someone. Just because you have spent one night with her, and you had a great time, does not mean you will feel the same after forty-eight or seventy-two hours together. If you are at her house for the weekend, make sure you are the perfect house guest. Make sure you clean up after yourself and offer to help if she is doing something. If she feels comfortable with having you there, and sees you can take care of yourself and respect her space, you will be invited back. If she is at your home, make sure she feels comfortable. By showing her where everything is, and encouraging her to treat your home like her home, she will feel a sense of belonging there.

As the nights over and weekend stays progress, start to be aware of how this would feel if it were a permanent living situation. She is! If staying at your home is becoming common, you want her to continue painting the picture of your bright future together. Offer to give her a small space in the bathroom for her regularly used products. If you want to make a really strong impact, show her she is the only one for you. Let her know you are enjoying your time together and you want her to continue coming over. Give her the opportunity to keep some spare feminine products underneath the bathroom sink in case of emergencies. To her it shows you are not interested in having any other woman at your home. First, because if another woman you brought home found that in your house she would leave quickly, calling you nasty names as she walked out the door. Second, because if anyone else saw it they would know she has become part of the household. Third, it is something very personal and necessary for her, and you are willing to have it in your home for her peace of mind. She will feel that you are ready to share your space and more of yourself with her. These gestures will help her feel more attached to you and your space.

I used to date a woman who would spend the weekends at my house. I sometimes worked for a few hours on Saturday mornings. So I would get up, get ready and give her a kiss goodbye before I left. After a few weekends of this I was amazed by what happened. I came home on a Saturday afternoon to find her waiting on the couch for me with a cocktail, and the entire house had been dusted and vacuumed. I was shocked. I told her how sweet I thought that was, but totally unnecessary. She explained to me she would normally do this in her house on Saturday mornings and, since she was staying at my house and felt so comfortable, she felt like she wanted to do the same thing here. I know that she did it because she cared about me and wanted to do something nice for me. She chose to clean because it is a comfortable habit for her to do every Saturday morning. She was feeling very comfortable in us sharing space together and that was her way of showing me.

If the weekend stays are primarily at her home, you want her to see how easy it would be for you to adapt to her space without much change for her. When you leave, take all of your belongings with you. Don't leave anything behind. Until you are invited to leave some convenient everyday items at her house, you shouldn't. When she offers for you to leave a toothbrush or extra shirt behind, you can gladly accept if you are ready. It shows you respect her space and are not trying to push or manipulate your way into her home. Until the time is right, your home is yours and her home is hers.

You might also find some new, unexpectedly enjoyable weekend rituals. I was dating a woman and we used to spend the weekends at her house. She used to get the Sunday paper delivered every week. I have not really been a newspaper reader in years. So, if we did not have plans first thing on Sunday morning, she would sit on the couch and read the newspaper. I would be doing something else and eventually we would start our day. One Sunday while she was sitting on the couch reading, she stretched her legs out on the couch. I decided to be cute and funny and sat down on the couch and began playing with her legs. She was smiling and giggling, trying to concentrate on her paper. I looked over and saw the comic section. I said to myself "Self, when was the last time you read the Sunday comics?" I realized it had been a long, long time. So I picked up the comics, stretched my legs out on the couch facing hers and started reading. She looked over at me and said, while smiling, "Oh, I see the comics are now more interesting than me." I responded "Not true, I can do both," and proceeded to play with her legs with my legs. I ended up reading half the newspaper while we sat and played footsie on the couch. The next weekend, the same thing happened. So in addition to a fun new ritual we started, I also discovered a renewed interest of my own-- reading the newspaper (but still enjoyed played with her legs while reading it). You might be surprised to refresh some old habits or find new ones by sharing space.

You will grow accustomed to each other's habits and rituals. Often the new habits and rituals created during these nighttime and weekend stays are created together. The more positive habits you experience together, the stronger the emotional bond that builds between you. The timing for this works well too because, generally, the weekends feel less stressful for people. So it's easier to reinforce positive feelings and emotions during this time.

It's very important to have a strong foundation for sharing intimate space, shared space and personal space. There's a fine line between feeling cared about and feeling suffocated. Communication is the key to gauge how you are both feeling and to make sure the time you spend together is positive and productive for the relationship. As time progresses and you spend more time together in a shared space, you will eventually decide if you want to take the next step. You should only consider the next step after you have ample time to truly learn about each other and each other's habits.

Bob and his current wife came up with a super fun dating ritual that most of us chose to adopt. Because they are both competitive people, a common phrase between them is "Wanna bet." Shortly after dating they came up with the amazing idea of the Win-Win bet. Each time they make a bet about something, the winner gets to choose what sexual position or escapade one partner gets to do with the other. What an awesome idea! It is truly a win-win situation. It is a very positive and fun game to play with your lover. It creates a less negative competitive relationship, they can bet all they want and everyone is a winner. I'm pretty sure all of us now enjoy gambling with our girlfriends and wives that much more.

Overnight stays offer other great opportunities to be romantic after you have left. Leave a note on her pillow for her to find later. Slip a note in her work briefcase or jacket pocket (just keep in mind someone else might be present when she finds it). And one of my personal favorites, and the one for which I have received much positive feedback, is a little dab of my cologne under her pillow, so when she goes to bed and wakes up, my scent is still there. Technically this could be regarded as marking your territory, but the purpose is different and it is much more effective than peeing on her pillow.

What do *you* think?

- Have you ever created fun new rituals with a woman you were dating?
- Have you ever left a note or cologne under a woman's pillow for her to find later?
- Have you ever thought about how the cleanliness of your home and/or car reflects on you?

WILLIAM WRIGHT

Step 8 - At The Sound of the Bell Come Out Disagreeing

"Anger is never without a reason, but seldom with a good one."

- Benjamin Franklin / Author, Inventor and Statesman

"I want a nice, clean fight. No low blows, and in the event of a knockdown, go to a neutral corner." Most of you will recognize this phrase as a simulation of the final instructions of a referee before a boxing match. An interesting fact I learned while researching this book--there is no absolute script for the final instructions before a professional fight. Each referee can create his own final instructions based on his own experiences. So, with that spirit of improvisation in mind: "I want a nice clean disagreement, watch your low blows and in the event of an emotional knockdown go to a neutral corner."

It is possible after you have been dating a woman for a while, you might encounter a difference of opinion (I know this is hard to believe). Bob stares at me and throws out a sarcastic "might." I don't like to refer to these deeply opinionated discussions as *fights*. I prefer to call them disagreements. There is a definitive reason for this.

> **Fight:** *a violent confrontation or struggle.*
>
> **Disagreement:** *a conflict or difference of opinion.*

When I am not agreeing with a woman and discussing the details, I don't want the connotation of violence or struggle involved in any way shape or form. Take a moment and speak those definitions out loud…Fight…Disagreement… You can feel yourself react emotionally to them both. Fighting generally creates a heightened, more emotional and very negative response. When I think of a fight, I think of a bloody knockdown, dragged out confrontation where the end result is one person standing over the other victorious while the other lies bloody, beaten and unconscious on the floor. Who would want this type of powerfully negative confrontation with someone they care about? A "disagreement" brings images of a calmer, more communicative discussion of ideas. It may involve an intense tone of voice or even an adversarial stare and, at worse, an agreement to disagree at the end of the debate. Both are left standing and hopefully a positive resolution is achieved.

Most of us have heard the phrase "Words can hurt like a fist." It is absolutely true. Most people don't think about how others react to their words. Words are very powerful tools and could be very positive or very negative. Words can also be used as a weapon. When you think of a battered spouse, you might think the physical abuse is the primary factor, but it's not. Often it is the mental abuse that creates the fear of physical violence. Of course the fear of the physical violence is present but the emotional manipulation can create as much fear and pain.

Nobody wants to have a confrontation with someone they care about. It is sometimes difficult enough just to verbalize how you are feeling about a certain subject. But if you feel like the other person does not understand you, the frustration levels escalate. This is multiplied by two if the other person is feeling misunderstood as well. When you break down a situation into smaller parts, you can get a better idea of the dynamics of what and why the situation is occurring. You have two people trying to explain their side of a situation so the other can understand. They are both emotionally charged, and are both feeling angry and misunderstood. The frustration builds because the other person does not just put their hand to their forehead and say "Oh, I get it." It is clear as glass to you, so why don't they just understand your point and give in? Well, we all have are our own individual feelings and experiences. In most cases, no two are identical.

Depending on your individual experience, each person has a different perspective on arguing. Did your family arguments start off with people talking and then slowly raising their voices until it became a yelling match? Were you taught that the person who yells the loudest is the one that gets heard? If this was the case you will instinctively and quickly escalate your volume during an argument, so you feel like the other person is hearing you. Or did your family talk to each other respectfully, and if someone got angry enough and raised their voice, it was considered disrespectful? The disrespected person would then walk away and no longer continue the discussion. If a person from each of these scenarios were to start arguing with each other, there would never be enough communication between them to resolve the issue. The moment one yelled, the other would leave, every time. You have to communicate, understand and set boundaries on how to argue. If you both understand how the other will hear what you have to say, the disagreements will be shorter and easier to resolve.

I remember witnessing an incident where two friends were having a disagreement at the dinner table. A bunch of us were sitting at the table preparing to eat when it started. It was a mild exchange of differing opinions between Shauna and Adam that was starting to escalate. As Adam started to raise his voice, he pushed his plate away to make more room for his arms to fly around while talking. He pushed his plate into Greg's plate, who was sitting across from him. I'm not sure if Adam did that by accident or on purpose. The hitting of the plates might have been for a sound effect or indication of his growing anger. When the plates collided Greg jumped up and with a violent outburst started screaming and threatening Adam for his outrageous behavior. Greg was furious with Adam for pushing things at the table and yelling and arguing at an inappropriate time and place. Greg's outburst came out of nowhere, but was obviously negative, passionate and hostile. After Greg's outburst, Adam walked away from the table and then left the house. When Greg finally calmed down, he apologized for his behavior, and he explained to us why he was so upset. When Greg was a child, arguing and plate-throwing during meals was a common occurrence at his house. He obviously did not like this behavior, and felt anger while it was going on. But as a child, he had no control over the situation. So, as this familiar scenario was playing out right in front of him, his initial reaction as an adult was to take control. He now felt that he could put a stop to the situation and chastise the person who was committing the offensive behavior. The point here is you never know what another person has experienced in their lives or their learned responses to specific situations. When anger escalates and disagreements turn into fighting, the overall outcome will be to push people apart. Greg's response to the fighting at the dinner table was significantly different then everyone else's. Other people might have experienced this same situation in the past, but had a different feeling or reaction to it at the time. Had the disagreement between Shauna and Adam been handled in a more communicative and mature method, their relationship might have been salvaged. In addition, the relationship between Greg and Adam might not have been strained beyond repair.

Starting from your first disagreement, you must lay down the ground rules for each of your fighting styles. Name calling and/or cursing at one another like kids in a schoolyard has no place in a healthy relationship based on mutual respect. How can you care about and respect someone whose only verbal communication during a disagreement is to spew a barrage of derogatory and hurtful names? It is childish, nonproductive, shows a lack of respect and will never result in a solution to the original problem. It's a destructive loss of self-control and only shows her you are not mature enough to have a relationship. On the reverse side of that coin, if she is the one who is saying these things to you, I would say it's time to start reevaluating your choice of women.

Some people have a harder time keeping their cool than others. It is vital that you give each other time and space to cool off if a disagreement enters the danger zone. A few years ago I was surprised to find myself deep in the danger zone with a former relationship. As we were shouting back and forth, my anger and stress were swiftly escalating. Knowing I needed to cool off, I went into the bedroom and closed the door to go away from her. Not knowing me very well, she pursued me into the bedroom. I asked her to leave me alone for a bit, while I calmed down. She was herself in the danger zone, and could not muster the self-control to stop yelling. Desperate to get some space, I walked to a park a couple of blocks away. I found a bench to sit on and took some deep, calming breaths. In my upset state, I did not notice that she had followed me. She appeared in front of me, just as confrontational as before I had left the house. My rage increased to such a level that I doubted my ability to control myself. I would never hit a woman, but my tense muscles seemed to have a mind of their own; my hands clenched into fists, my arms shook and my voice trembled. I jumped up and stared at her with deep, cold, dead eyes. I miraculously mustered up the self-control to say, "If you don't walk away from me right now, I am going to do something we are both going to regret for the rest of our lives!" An ominous and absolute silence descended upon us. Time itself seemed to hesitate. She stared into my eyes, and pondered her next words. I prayed she would just turn and walk away because although I had never struck a woman, I felt caged and pushed to my limits. I was not sure I could control my rage any longer. She opened her mouth to speak and then stopped, closed her lips and walked away. Discussing it later, she admitted that she knew she was pushing my threshold level of control, especially by following me and ignoring my requests to let me calm down for a while before we continued our conversation. She also confessed that she had planned to continue her tirade, until she saw the vacant look in my eyes. I learned that I could exercise self-control, and I learned that she cared more about fighting than about me. Needless to say I ended the relationship immediately afterward. Why would I want to continue a relationship with someone who had so little regard for my feelings and provoked such negative reactions?

Another thing to be aware of is setting patterns for disagreements. It takes twenty-one days to break a bad habit or to create a good habit. With awareness, you can avoid setting up patterns of particular events, days or situations which will reliably generate an argument. We often unconsciously create scenarios to enable an argument because we don't know more effective ways to express our needs and desires.

Try to keep your disagreements as brief as possible. A long drawn out conversation only deepens the emotional attachment to the topic. If someone needs time to calm down before continuing, you must respect their style of disagreeing. You can continue a little later when they are calmer and more receptive to a resolution. Don't bring other participants into your arguments. It only complicates the situation and the agenda of others might not be the same as yours. Ultimately the *way* you resolve your differences is more important than the specific resolution. Healthy and respectful discussions in which both you and your partner feel heard and empathized with will make your relationship stronger. Avoid going to bed angry because your subconscious mind will ruminate upon negative and contentious thoughts while you sleep. When you wake up in the morning, you will feel drained and agitated, and the new day will deepen your anger and resentment. It is difficult to start your morning feeling positive, energized and ready to take on your day when all the negative feelings that have grown bigger during the night are staring you in the face.

There is a theory that angry sex or make up sex can be more intense than your regular sexual activity. Though it *can* be, that is not the answer to diminishing intimacy. I have known some friends who used to argue constantly. It did not matter who was around, or where they were. They would get very heated and say some very cruel things to each other. Of course, if other people were around, this would make for a very uncomfortable situation. The day after a few such rounds I would ask one of them if everything was all right and if they had resolved the issue. Inevitably, one of them would say, "Yeah, we worked it out and the makeup sex last night was worth it." One day after a huge blowout at a large gathering, I called my friend to check on him. He told me they were getting divorced. She had decided she did not want to continue their constantly angry and hurtful lifestyle. They had grown so accustomed to the behavior that they had based their intimacy and sex life on it. You are better off seeking out new, interesting and positive ways to keep your sex life exciting, than using a negative reinforcement which will eventually lead to the end of a relationship.

Disagreements are a part of life. They can be beneficial if you learn from them. Listen to what someone says to you during an argument. If you pay attention you will learn much more about what they think, how they feel, how they process information and how they relate information to others. If you understand their processes better, you can more easily relate to the information and feelings they are trying to convey to you. We don't always say what we mean or mean what we say. Learn how to understand your partner's communication style, both verbal and physical. It will go a very long way toward shortening and preventing disagreements.

What do *you* think?

- Do you typically disagree with your woman in a respectful, constructive manner?
- Have you ever had a disagreement with a woman where one of you walked out shouting?
- How did you finally resolve the disagreement?

WILLIAM WRIGHT

Step 9 – The Merger – Moving in Together

"Thousands of candles can be lighted from a single candle, and the life of the candle will not be shortened. Happiness never decreases by being shared."

- Buddha / Sage and Founder of Buddhism

So the time has come. After meeting, dating and spending time together you have decided to take the next step. After ample discussion and deep thought, you have decided to merge your worlds and take a *test run* before you take the plunge. You're thinking, "Hey, I didn't say I was going to marry her, just move in with her." I am here to inform you that when you both agreed to take the next step and live together, she is thinking this is the prequel to the rest of your lives. Women don't move in with a partner just to have a roommate. Women move in with a man to test the waters with an expectation of future commitment. So make sure you are ready mentally and emotionally to start sharing your life, and are serious about the future potential.

Make sure you are in agreement for the right reasons. If you agree to move in together because you think you can save money, its closer to your work, you will have more sex or it's just something new to try, you are going to be sadly disappointed. Not only that, but you are going down the road to misery, frustration and heartache. When she realizes your motives are not the same, your living situation will get uncomfortable and ugly very quickly. So make sure you have thought this through before making this decision.

If she has children your role will be changing in regards to them as well. You will become a full-time parent figure in their lives. Obviously, she is comfortable with this; otherwise she would not have invited you to share their lives. Make certain to discuss your role regarding her children. Topics should include care, raising and discipline. Like any parent figures, if you are living with her and her children, you both need to be on the same page when it comes to the kids. If you don't agree on child rearing issues and discipline, more discussion is vital before you move in. Raising children can be very rewarding, but very strenuous on a relationship (communication is vital). You will become a daily influence and take part in their welfare and well-being, so make certain you are prepared for this added responsibility. Embrace the experience and have fun with it.

Perhaps you are the one in the relationship that has children. If you do have children make sure you are moving in together for the right reasons. If you're looking for a mother for your children, want to alleviate some financial burdens or think it might just be fun for a while, rethink your decision. Children have a very fragile emotional development. Some will attach to a parent figure easily, and others will act out to convey their discontent. Either way, you could be in for an emotional roller coaster you did not bargain for. If she is the woman of your dreams, you will work through any obstacles you encounter to create a harmonious and long lasting family. If, on the other hand, this is destined to be a short-term relationship and your reasons for moving in together are frivolous, you will be the direct cause of much emotional turmoil for your children and yourself. Your priority should be your children. I also suggest you both sit down together and discuss with the children what you are planning so they feel as though they are included in this new extended family.

Finances are another very important discussion to have prior to moving in together. Money is the most common cause of relationship problems. Most people have very strong but different thoughts, feelings and experiences with money. The emotions tied to money, whether positive or negative, run deep in the subconscious. Experiences with finances vary so much within individuals. It is vital to decide beforehand how you are going to handle monthly bills (electric, gas, cable), savings, vacations, unexpected costs, kids lunch money, household repairs, new furniture, etc. Often people find conversations about money, as difficult, if not more difficult, than talking about sex. Money is viewed as personal as your deepest, darkest secrets. But as we discussed earlier, these difficult conversations can strengthen your relationship and alleviate future obstacles. However you decide to divide the household finances and responsibilities, each person should be aware and agree upon what their contribution will be.

When you are moving in together for the right reasons, it is a very exciting time. It is truly a growth opportunity for you as an individual and as a couple. As individuals we constantly evolve throughout our lives (well, that is the idea). We go from children with our own bedrooms, to students living in a dorm or sharing a house. We eventually get our own apartment and decorate it the way we like. We move on to owning a home with more space and more personal furnishings that suit our taste. Generally the way we decorate and keep our personal space defines us. And because we are all individuals, everyone's personal space is a little different. We generally grow into our space, meaning the more space we have the more things we find to fill it. As a result, over the years we have accumulated a lot of junk; some in storage boxes, some shoved to the back of closets, some in the garage, and some, like Bob, might still have some boxes in his parent's garage. As anyone discovers as they are packing, people collect a lot of stuff (and I phrased that nicely) that they don't even remember they have.

Being that you are about to consolidate your "stuff" with someone else's "stuff" it is going to get very crowded, very quickly. This is where you get to mature as individuals and let go of your past "stuff." As we take new steps in our lives, we need to shed old parts of our lives to continue forward. When a snake sheds its skin periodically, it does so in order to grow. Afterwards, the snake's new skin is healthy and rejuvenated. You will wow her with your maturity as you are able to get rid of the items from your past that have no use in your future. Do you really still need your super cool poster collection, tennis racket with no strings, framed velour picture of dogs playing poker, yoyo collection, bong you used in college, or bowling ball that you never bowl with? And of course all adult magazine type literature you just read for the articles must go. Yes, you must give up the ADULT LITERATURE! Right now all the guys are nodding their heads in agreement, except for Javier. I think he has a hidden stash.

If it makes you feel any better she is going to have to give up her accumulated "stuff" too. She will part with her high school field hockey stick, stuffed animal collection, pink curtains, Precious Moments collection, bong she used in college, extra frilly dishware and all her EROTIC ROMANCE NOVELS.

Now that you are living together, don't fall into the comfort trap. You have done a great job thus far to have her fall in love with you. Don't backtrack now. You now have to show her what a great life partner you can be, and how having you there benefits her. Make sure you are doing all the household things you would normally do living on your own. Don't get lazy and start leaving messes around the house, expecting her to clean up after you. Don't rely on her to do all the cooking and cleaning up after meals. Joe makes a good point: "What if I never cooked before? I ate out all the time and she knows it?" If you never cooked, then you split the responsibility as you would any other, sometimes she might cook and sometimes you take her out for dinner. If you really want to be the king of all wooing, learn how to cook something and surprise her. She will melt like the butter in your recipe. Make sure you are appreciative when she does do things for you like cooking. Never stop saying "Thank you" (verbal) and showing your appreciation (actions). Clear off the table and help her with the dishes. If she feels like you are a team and she is appreciated, she will go far beyond your expectations to keep you happy.

Now that you live together, there are many more opportunities to create audio, visual, emotional and physical cues throughout your home. Just as you were creating positive emotional anchors while you were dating, you want to continue this through your entire relationship. What you might not realize is that as you are creating positive emotional responses for her, they will be affecting you too. This is a good thing because it is part of what makes you love her too. She will remember a romantic candlelit dinner in the kitchen, cuddling on the couch watching a love story on TV, a relaxing bath together, having a cup of coffee on the patio staring at the moonlight, sitting on the floor exchanging holiday gifts, etc. You can have pictures around of the two of you having fun. Play songs you both like to listen to. Dance with her in the kitchen or massage her shoulders while she is cooking dinner. Figure out what works for you, but never forget to give her the attention she deserves. You don't want her to forget about you.

Another trap that some men fall into is the, "I have a woman, so it doesn't matter what I look like" snafu. She fell in love with you and the way you look. If all of sudden your habits change and you gain fifty pounds, she is going to notice. If you always shaved every day and now you go every three days, she will notice. Maybe you were a nice dresser and now gym shorts and flip flops are your daily uniform. She will notice. Make sure to continue the habits that make you the person she fell in love with. Would you want her to gain fifty pounds, not shave and wear baggy gym shorts every day? I don't think so. If you are a gym enthusiast, then continue going. If you are a meticulous groomer, keep grooming. You can make changes in your life when you live with someone, but make sure they are positive changes that are good for you. And she will notice the positive changes too. She is already in love with you, so the positive changes you make in your life will make you that much more irresistible to her.

People are generally creatures of habit. They create patterns in their lives that they tend to follow. When you start to share your life with someone, new patterns are unintentionally created. Be mindful that the patterns unfolding are the way you want to live your life, and that she is happy with them as well. A new pattern that will be created is your sex life. Everyone has a different idea of how many times a day, week or month they like to have sex. This *does* need to be addressed. For instance, perhaps you like to have sex every day, but she only likes to have sex every other day. If you start out being intimate every other day, that will become the norm. The pattern will set in and will be very difficult to change. Remember it takes twenty-one days to make or break a habit, so patience and communication are the keys. Focus on the outcome that is positive for you both.

All the women I have been in a relationship with understood I am a sex-every-day kind of guy. From the beginning of our courtship, I made it clear I am a very physical person. I enjoy sex and I also enjoy pleasing my woman. I assume it was one of the things about me they fell in love with. So when I moved in, it was natural to have sex every day. I did not deviate from the pattern and it stuck. I have lived with several women, and with each one of them, our pattern was to have sex at least once a day. Be honest about what makes you happy. Discuss what makes her happy, and what you both expect when you move in together. Have conversations about expectations and how to make living together the best experience it can be for you both you. These conversations will take her emotional bond with you to a higher level. If she feels you are being honest, opening up to her and willing to work to make the relationship successful, she will do everything in her power to make it work. She will even compromise more than you will to fulfill her own emotional expectations.

> *"She is not there to serve you, you be there to support her."*

Remember living with someone is a partnership, not a dictatorship. Make sure you are keeping up with your contribution and responsibilities in the house. However you choose to divide up chores, make sure you do your part. The best way to think about this is: "She is not there to serve you, you be there to support her." Bob excitedly shares, "I once served a woman breakfast in bed." Then I ask Bob, "How many times did that woman serve *you* breakfast in bed?" He answered with a smile "several times." My response is "That is my point." If you treat a woman like a princess, most times she will treat you like the king. I don't mean this in a sexist way at all. In my experience when a woman feels loved, respected, protected and appreciated she will return those feelings tenfold. When you do your part for the household, you make yourself indispensable. She wants you to be there, and if you continue those positive behaviors, she always will.

Decorating your space together will require patience and determination. I will never forget the story Jeff told us about living four months without a coffee table because he and his girlfriend could not agree on anything they saw. If you are one of those guys who doesn't really care how the house is decorated, this will be easy for you (and I am jealous). If there is a particular area you would like a certain way, then you can propose that she do whatever she likes throughout the home, but that you would like to decorate that particular spot. As long as this is really what you want, this could be an effective solution. Chances are she will love you that much more for it. For those of you like me and Jeff, it is a bit more complicated. This is the first of many important decisions you will make together. It is also another opportunity to create a bond on a different level. When you do find that perfect couch or coffee table that you both like and the purchase is made, you have just made a "WE" decision. In her mind you just made an emotional purchase together. She will feel it as an emotional bond and a commitment to the relationship. I have seen a woman cry and profess her deepest love after the delivery of a new dining table we picked out together. Just remember, compromise is the key. The happier she is, the happier you are.

Just because you live together now, does not mean you stop wooing her. It means there are more opportunities to make her fall more madly in love with you. You are now spending more time together, and the romance should increase. For Jeff, keeping the romance means "Never stop kissing hello and goodbye." And I have seen him and his wife hold true to that sentiment. Doug says if he leaves early in the morning and she is asleep, he will go in and kiss her goodbye. If she is awake, he kisses her goodbye before walking out the door. When either one of them comes home the first thing they do is look for the other to give them a kiss. What an awesome concept! He is constantly kissing the woman he loves. How romantic is that? They are also constantly reinforcing the bond of intimacy and physical contact. You can tell when they are around each other how comfortable and natural it is for them to be close to each other. They are always holding hands, wrapping their arms around each other's waist, or just smiling at each other from across a room. For Doug, romance is the little surprises he and his wife like to spring on each other. For example, Doug's wife often hands him a margarita when he comes home on a Friday night while wearing just her very short silk robe (don't tell her he told us about that). He likes to surprise her with flowers, and he leaves little notes in her briefcase for her to find at work. Sometimes she comes home after a tough day at work to find a hot bath waiting for her. But their favorite thing is snuggling up together in bed on Saturday mornings before starting their day. This pattern started when they moved in together. Come up with your own romantic ideas, no matter how big or small. Keep dating her even though you live with her. This will allow you both to experience the best of both worlds.

Bob is finding great joy with his current wife, who is also a sports fan. They both like to watch baseball and football. They discovered they both really enjoyed watching games and being intimate. So they decided to mix the two. Now they look forward to half time and the seventh inning stretch as much as the games themselves. This works great for them unless they are in the living room on Super Bowl Sunday with a dozen other people (awkward).

A big adjustment you will have to get used to is the daily intricacies of sharing your life. When you live on your own you come and go whenever you want, and never have to consult with anyone but yourself. When you live with someone there is a different respect for time. Someone else is now aware of your schedule. It's not that they are monitoring you; they just have knowledge of where you are supposed to be and when. And it is a respect issue about time, and her concern for you. This is not a bad thing, but might take some getting used to. Before a friend might have called you at work and asked if you wanted to have dinner that night. You'd say "Sure, see you at seven." After hanging out for dinner and a couple of drinks you'd head home. Now, if you did the same exact thing, you would be getting a phone call by 7:30 asking if you are okay. Once again, not a bad thing, but you are now sharing your schedule with someone who knows you are usually home by seven. So, if you don't show when you would normally be there, they will start to worry. Perhaps she might have started dinner in anticipation of your arrival. She will probably feel angry about her wasted effort when she finds out you ate elsewhere. You don't have to feel confined by this. It will take some communication and consideration until it becomes natural. By communicating with her, and taking into account her time, you will find she is very appreciative to know you are okay wherever you are. Give her a call or text (which you should be doing anyway) during the day just to let her know you are meeting your friend for dinner. It is not a lot of trouble. It's being considerate and respectful. I always suggest looking at a situation from both sides of the fence. If you were to cook dinner for your significant other who was late, and you had not heard from her, wouldn't you be worried? If you were not worried, that could indicate a different problem! Generally, if a woman feels you are taking her feelings into consideration, it is one more reason to love you and brag to her friends.

What do *you* think?

- Have you ever moved in with a woman and it was not successful?
- Have you ever experienced financial matters as a source of conflict? How did you solve the issue?

Step 10 – Don't Pop the Question, Plan the Question

"Don't marry the person you think you can live with; marry only the individual you think you can't live without."

- James C. Dobson / Author and Psychologist

"Get inside her head, so you can blow her mind."

Right now, all the guys at the table have that "man grin" on their faces. It is the "Sooo… you're going to pop the question, take the plunge, tie the knot" look. For some reason every man gets that same facial expression when they talk about getting married. The grin might mean different things for different men but, oddly enough, it always looks the same. Bob takes a long sip of his drink and asks anxiously "How are you going to ask her?"

Just about every guy wants to come up with the most romantic proposal of all time. They want to speak like Shakespeare and act out the scene like Sir Lawrence Olivier. Often what happens is quite the contrary. Either you can't think of something you want to do, the plan becomes to elaborate, or they just give up. Jeff jokes,

"Let's have a show of hands. Who thinks the marriage proposal is for them? No hands up? You guys are smarter than you look." He is correct. The marriage proposal is not about you, what you would like to do or where you would like to do it. It should be about HER!

We have all heard some creative ways men have proposed. How many stories have you heard about unimaginative, dull and lazy ways men have popped the question? Not too many. You don't hear about those, because women don't boast about them. They barely talk about it with their friends, and never talk about it in their future. Don't be that guy. You have been doing great so far. Your woman loves and adores you. Give her something that's special to her, that she will want to talk about for a lifetime. The cigar band on her finger, while on one knee at a local restaurant, only works in Vegas. Probably because everyone is so drunk, it does not matter to her until morning when she remembers what happened.

While doing some research I discovered the enormous number of websites pertaining to marriage proposals. Some made sense, and many were just ridiculous. After looking at many sites, I began to notice a pattern. Three out of four women did not prefer the way their husband proposed to them. And many surveys reported only twenty eight percent of women were really surprised by the proposal. The other seventy two percent played along so not to hurt their soon to be fiancé's feelings. They learned about the proposals in many different ways: friends, family, and outsiders helping with the big plan or sometimes just by the behavior of her boyfriend. I was not shocked that only ten percent of women would be fine with a proposal on a jumbotron at a sporting event. Unless the woman is a die hard team fan, he was just trying to kill two birds with one stone. Men have gone to extremes to impress the woman they love into marrying them. One guy jumped off a building while his girlfriend stood by horrified. His miraculous return at the end of a bungee cord was followed by his proposal. Whaaat? They compile lists of the best and worst ways to propose. The common factor in all the worst ways to propose was that the guy found a way for him to have some fun, or make it all about him, while he handed his girlfriend a ring.

Keep in mind you have a goal here. Your goal is to make this proposal an event she will never forget, in a way that touches her so deeply that she will talk about it for the rest of her life. Also, you want her to say "Yes." It might sound like a daunting task but it's not as hard as you think.

Start by finding what has meaning for her. What does she enjoy doing? Where does she enjoy going? Is she very family-oriented? If so, how could you involve her family in the proposal? Is she very close to her friends? Could they be given a supportive role in the event? A word of caution, though, the more people who know the better chance she will find out. You will have to get inside her head to blow her mind. If she is shy, you don't want to propose in the middle of a crowded dance club or big event. She will feel self-conscious, and probably not enjoy the moment. If she is very outgoing, you may consider asking her at a party or bigger event where she will get more attention. Think about her personality.

Dan, a guy I used to work with, came up with a very impressive idea for his proposal. I had to pat him on the back when he told me. He was dating a woman who loved to hike. He very much enjoyed hiking as well. They hiked together in many different areas and terrains. One day he asked her if she was up for a challenge. He wanted to hike the biggest mountain they had ever hiked. They were proficient hikers, but this was bigger than they were used to. She agreed to give it a try, and they made plans to go in two weeks. When they arrived at the trail they both looked up at the top, then at each other. They smiled at each other and started up the trail. It was a hot, summer day which made the hike more difficult. Halfway up he could she was starting to get a little fatigued. He asked her if she wanted to stop and head back down. He knew she is a very determined person and would not want to quit. About three quarters of the way up, she looked tired but still determined. He offered some words of encouragement, reminding her of how awesome she was going to feel when she got to the top and accomplished her goal of climbing this big mountain. When they reached the summit she ran to highest part of the peak, raised her arms and yelled in celebration. Glowing with pride and pumped up with adrenaline, she walked over to a big rock overhanging the peak to look down. As she looked all around, all she could see was sky. It was the ultimate rush for her. She shouted to Dan to come see the incredible view. When she turned around Dan was right behind her holding out an open ring box with a nice ring. She stood speechless for several long seconds. Then she blurted out "Yes! Yes I will marry you." He never got a chance to ask her. . She dropped to her knees, sobbing with joy and elation. He then took her hand and put the ring on her finger. On the way down she told him that this was better than she had ever expected the best day of her life to be. It was also better than the best marriage proposal she could have ever imagined. Dan told me she loves to tell people the story every opportunity she gets.

I am not saying you must climb a mountain to propose. Dan just wanted to make sure she was in a place with special meaning. Try to get inside her head. It's easy to think of where you would want to propose, but make sure it has symbolic significance for both of you. I once dated a girl who loved to sleep. If the opportunity arose on a weekend afternoon, she would relish the idea of taking a nap. I always thought if I was going to propose to her I would slip the ring on her finger while she was sleeping (she was a heavy sleeper) so that she could be surprised and wake up with a ring on her finger.

Just give it some deep thought and Find Her Sweet Spot. I am sure you will think of a way to blow her mind!

What do *you* think?

- Do you notice that other women excitedly tell the story of their proposal, but your wife never does?
- Have you ever considered coming up with an idea that would blow her mind and propose again, renewing your vows?
- Can you connect her natural likes/personality to your brainstorming of ideas of how you might architect your re-proposal?

Step 11 – And They Lived Happily Ever After – Far From the End

"If you don't design your own life plan, chances are you'll fall into someone else's plan. And guess what they have planned for you? Not much."

- Jim Rohn / Author and Motivational Speaker

How many times have you seen a cute elderly couple in their seventies, eighties or even their nineties, slowly walking arm in arm down the street. They are walking at a slow pace but in unison. They talk to each other, smile and laugh while occasionally patting each other on the arm. Everyone's first response is "Awwww, they are so cute." Even the manliest of men will soften a bit at the site of long time lovers sharing a stroll together in their golden years. Usually their next thought is *"How did they manage to stay together for all those years and still be so in love?"*

You and your new wife met, dated, fell in love, and moved in together. Great job! You worked hard together and you achieved your goal of Finding Her Sweet Spot. Achieving your goal of finding the right woman, falling in love and spending the rest of your life with her is not much different then achieving any of your life's goals. You stayed focused, worked hard for want you want, gave something back and now you can enjoy the benefits. But like anything in life, when you achieve what you want you still have to be willing to put forth effort to keep it. Just because you are married does not mean that everything you were doing to woo her before getting married just stops. It's been said "Life is a journey, not a destination." I believe that to be true. You have started your lives together and there is still a long way to go. Perhaps your next goal to achieve is to be that cute elderly couple walking arm in arm through the park. The people you pass will smile and wonder how you managed to stay in love all those years.

As we age, we encounter new challenges in the different stages of our lives. It could be professional, financial, medical or emotional. The difference now is you can deal with things together. You can now share your problems with each other. Being able to rely on your spouse has many benefits most people do not even think about. For instance, imagine you have this big problem (let's call it a couch) and it is a huge burden to carry around. It is very heavy and you find you are getting tired from lugging it around with you everywhere you go. It makes you feel tired quickly, wears you down and makes you feel very unhappy. Now imagine you have told your spouse about this problem (the couch) and because she truly loves you, she offers to help you carry the couch. Now you are combining your talents, skills, and creativity. You are sharing your strength, and working on the problem together. It is not my couch, or your couch. It is *our* couch. How much lighter and easier is it to carry your burden with half the weight? How much better is it to have someone helping and supporting this heavy load? At some point you will solve your problem and toss the couch aside. By working together you will have both become stronger, more bonded to each other and better at carrying furniture together.

Bob is telling us a story about a coworker and friend who fell into a terrible way shortly after he got married. Jordan had been married for only two years when the department in the company he worked for started laying people off. When Jordan first married, his financial situation was very stable and on an upswing. Jordan's wife had a job, but he made much more money and their lifestyle was based primarily on his income. After about one year of marriage, his company started having trouble and his sales were decreasing. His income started dropping dramatically. Jordan had been very self sufficient his entire life and didn't feel as though he should share his financial issues with his wife. He did not want to worry her or feel like he could not provide for their lifestyle. After almost a year of barely hanging on to his job, the financial burden became overwhelming. He could see it was affecting him and his relationship with his wife. He was feeling crushed by the accumulating debt, and covering the monthly bills became difficult. He was irritable all the time and starting to resent his wife every time she spent a dollar. Keep in mind she was totally unaware of what was going on. He took care of the finances on his own.

One night after an ordinary dinner they were loading the dishwasher together as they always do. His wife remarked how they needed to call a repairman for the dishwasher because it was starting to leak. Or they could just get a new one which would be more energy efficient as well. Jordan snapped. His eyes got wide, his lips pursed lightly together and his body got very stiff. He started shouting out of nowhere, "This is it! I can't take it anymore!" He went on a verbal tirade about how she did not understand what it takes to the run the household and maintain the lifestyle they were leading. He continued yelling that she didn't understand the value of money and that she was frivolous. He exclaimed that he worked way too hard to be in this situation, and that he would have been better off financially if he had stayed single. He continued in the same vein for several more minutes. At last, his rant ended, leaving him physically and emotionally exhausted. His final words were, "I want a divorce." His wife just stood there like a deer staring into headlights. She was confused, feeling attacked and emotionally on guard. In a shaky voice she asked him, "What are talking about? What is going on here?" Jordan stammered ineffectually for a minute, and then fell silent. He took a deep breath, and finally shared how grim their financial situation was. She just sat there in shock, as he explained how deep a hole they were in. Then she began to yell about how he had kept this information from her for so long. The argument continued for hours, with both of them feeling scared of the future, betrayed and blaming each other. I am sorry to say that within a couple of months they lost their house, their savings were gone, their credit was destroyed and they did get a divorce. This is a perfect example of allowing your spouse to help you carry the couch (share your problems). Due to a lack of communication for so long, and the deep feelings of betrayal, they could not repair the marriage. The sad part of this scenario is it did not have to happen.

We need to continue to woo our wives. One way we do that is by sharing the good, the bad and the ugly that occurs in our everyday lives. Obstacles can either weaken, or strengthen your bond. If you choose to face and conquer obstacles together, you can create new, positive emotional bonds. You both have obstacles and should depend on each other for support and assistance. Young Jeff blurts out, "I disagree. I am the man, I am supposed to protect her, and she is not supposed to take on my problems." Doug, the oldest of the group, explains to Jeff that yes, he is the man and most men feel like they should protect their wife and that is a good thing. But it is very chauvinistic, especially these days, to think your wife could not handle or be helpful with a problem. He further explained how in his many years of marriage his wife had become his most trusted advisor, as well as a lover. She also helps him move furniture up and down the stairs of life. He claims "Sometimes she is the voice of reason, sometimes she plays the devils advocate and certain times she is the key idea woman to complete my master plan." He ends with a villainous laugh and plays with the tip of an imaginary moustache. Bob asks Jeff, "Were you ever thinking of asking your friend's advice about a situation and thought, 'I just don't know if he can handle it'?" Jeff doesn't have to ponder his answer: "No. If I ask for a buddy's advice, why would I think he couldn't handle it?" Bob said "Exactly. Why wouldn't you ask your best friend for advice?" Jeff stares at him for a moment, thinking and exclaims, "Wow, that's deep!" We all look at each other and burst out laughing. We all agree that Jeff has a lot to learn, but he'll get there.

Your wife should be one of your best friends as well as your lover. We all have friends we have met over our lifetime. Some we met as children, as adolescents, and some as adults. Friendships evolve and dissolve throughout our lives. We change where we live, our jobs and we all grow as individuals at a unique pace. The friends you have now will hopefully be in your lives for a very long time, but some may not. You and your wife vowed to stay together until death due you part. I never made that vow with my elementary school buddies while playing ball in the schoolyard. And if I had that would have been a little awkward. Wouldn't it make sense to be sure to choose your best friend as the person you plan to spend the rest of your life? Some decisions in life really are that simple. There is a theory called Occam's Razor. It states that the simplest explanation is usually the right one. If you ask most people "Who is your best friend?" The answer is usually someone they have known for a while and feel very close to. If you ask about their spouse, they will usually respond "Bob is my best friend, she is my wife." How often do you hear of best friends getting a divorce? Just something to think about.

I am not implying you should replace your male best friend or any of your friends. We all have a group of friends we hang out with. We also have friends we have known for many years and might be very close because of all the experiences we have shared together. Often people will have one or two best buddies that know you as well as you know yourself. Perhaps you even grew up together. These friends are very valuable to us and it's difficult to picture our lives without them. Imagine your best friend. Now imagine if you never spoke to or hung out with them again. It's hard to even think about the impact of not talking to someone who you have truly counted on, turned to for support and shared so many of your crazy life experiences with. Yet you hear of marriages being discarded over some of the most ridiculous circumstances, things you would never consider breaking up a friendship over. Make your wife part of that group. Your wife should be one of your best friends with whom you share your life experiences. The one you're talking to when you say "Remember when we…" Eventually you will have a lifetime of stories, good and bad, of the crazy things you went through together. And you get to have great sex with her too. Woo hoo!

There is an old joke where one guy asks another guy who is thinking about getting married "Would you rather get married or get a tattoo?" The guy thinks about it for a moment and answers "I would rather get married. A tattoo is so permanent." Your beliefs guide your actions much more than you may be aware. Many people today don't think of marriage as a permanent institution. They figure they will give it a try, and if it doesn't work, you just divorce. If that's the way you think, why get married? If you don't believe it is permanent, chances are it won't be. Our beliefs determine how we look at any situation. Our beliefs determine the actions we take toward the outcome of a situation or event. So the outcome of the event will usually end in the way we expect because we have taken actions that will cause the outcome we want. It's called a "Self Fulfilling Prophecy." Jeff looks at me with his head cocked to the side like a confused puppy. He stares at me blankly. "What?" You subconsciously take actions to support your thoughts. For instance, if you truly believe a dance club is a great place to meet women; chances are you will meet women there. You will subconsciously take all the actions necessary because you believe the outcome will match your beliefs. If you think you will not meet women at dance clubs, you won't. You might take actions but subconsciously sabotage yourself to match your belief. So, even if you want to meet women at the club, if your beliefs tell you that you're not going to; you won't. It's the story we tell ourselves.

We all have a set of beliefs that have been taught to us from birth. It is our beliefs that guide us in our actions. Not all of our beliefs are accurate, positive or even make any reasonable sense. We learned these beliefs from someone else's experiences. The great news is that we can pick and choose what our beliefs are. We can consciously examine our beliefs and discard the ones which are not currently serving our goals. If you believe women aren't strong enough for you to share problems with, it will be difficult for you to do so. If you believe that one disagreement with your wife indicates that the entire marriage was a mistake, then you will not pursue a positive resolution to the disagreement, and the marriage will, in reality, fail. Your beliefs will subconsciously create the actions to prove your belief. Regardless of what you believe, you are right. You brain will create for you the reality you envision. You can see why it is important to really examine your belief system to ensure you achieve a positive and desirable outcome for your marriage and in ALL areas of your life.

I can't stress enough the importance of setting positive goals in your life. If you ask the most successful people in any field they will share with you how goal setting was essential to their achievements. We all have goals in life. Negative people call them impossible dreams. Positive people focus on their goals, write them down, break them into manageable steps, look at them regularly and take actions to achieve what they want. As a couple, goal setting is important too. Often it is the understanding of what you both want for your future. A goal could be the vacation you want to take. What do you have to plan to achieve this? Perhaps it's researching where you both want to go, putting money aside for the trip (x amount per week), planning time off from work, and answering basic questions such as: For how long will you go? What do you want to do there? Whom will you visit? Who will take care of the dog? Remember goal setting should be as specific as possible. Maybe you currently rent an apartment but would like to eventually purchase a home. When you and your partner co-create the goal, and take action together to bring it to fruition, you greatly increase the likelihood of success. If you are both participating in actualizing the goal then you are not only rewarded with the achievement itself, but you also strengthen your bond and take the relationship to the next level of trust and intimacy. This will give you the confidence to aim for even higher and larger goals. It can also become one of the great stories you love to tell people-- "Remember when we...?"

We still need to set individual goals. They are what make us feel good about ourselves and strive for continuous growth. But sit down together and discuss your goals for the future like a one, five, ten, twenty, and even a fifty year goal. Just by setting a fifty year goal you have increased your chances for successful, long-term, marital bliss. Most people don't even think one year ahead, much less what they would like their life to be like in fifty years with their loving wife. What you can picture you can achieve. If you ever had a daydream you understand. You are somewhere and your mind starts to wander. You get this clear picture in your head of something you have been thinking about. You can see it very vividly and it feels absolutely real. All of a sudden you hear a noise or something catches your attention, and you shake your head back to reality. That's usually when you realize you were daydreaming. It felt real and left you with a good feeling. If you can picture something that clearly, you can achieve it. So if you can picture your life that far ahead with the woman you love, you can make it happen.

When you first get married, it is just the two of you starting a new life. If you decide to have children, you take on new responsibilities. For a minimum of the next eighteen years you will be sharing the daily requirements of raising that child in your home every day. Children require a lot of love, attention and time. You will also have the opportunity to create many positive emotional bonds together as parents and a family. Unfortunately, I have seen many marriages fizzle because the parents do not make any time for themselves. Their lives become their children and they lose their identities as husbands, wives and lovers. I am not saying you should not give all you can to your children, but they have to grow as individuals and so do adults. Be aware not to lose your identity as lovers. Make certain you schedule date nights, intimacy and just time to talk. Support and replenish your bond with each other by nurturing a healthy sex life and having regularly scheduled fun together. Make this a priority. This may mean that you have to schedule in sex time or hire a babysitter and go to a hotel (which could be fun). Fun fact: Research shows having sex at least twice a week reduces your risk of a heart attack. Who knew? It's enjoyable and good for your health.

What you don't want is to let twenty years slip by without nurturing your marriage. If you only focus on raising your kids, then you may discover that when they go off to college, you are alone in the house with a stranger. If you find you have nothing in common and no bond whatsoever with your wife, it can be difficult to recover what you have lost. This a common reason for divorces after twenty plus years of marriage. You have both dedicated your time and energy to career, kids and everyday life, but have drifted so far apart from your spouse that there is nothing left to keep you together. This is very sad and so unnecessary after spending a bulk of your lives together. Just because you have kids, you should still woo your wife. As I indicated in the beginning, wooing her and Finding Her Sweet Spot is a lifelong enjoyment. When the kids are gone and it's just the two of you again, you want it to be better than it was in the beginning. As long as you keep that bond constantly growing, she will love you forever. Now you can continue to work on achieving your fifty year goals together.

Imagine you are walking down a crowded street on a nice warm spring afternoon. Walking toward you, arm in arm, is an elderly couple in their eighties. They are walking at a slow pace but in unison. They talk to each other, smile and laugh while occasionally patting each other on the arm. You think "Awwww, they are so cute." You find it very heartwarming to see a couple who have shared their long lives together and are so happy and obviously still in love. As you walk closer to them you can hear them laughing and you can get a better look at their wrinkled, smiling, sweet faces. Imagine how you feel when you walk right up to them to find that sweet older couple that is so much in love, is YOU and your loving wife.

What do *you* think?

- Do you and your wife communicate freely about your feelings?
- What's in it for you to meet her emotional needs and her desire for true intimacy?

Step 12 – Appreciate Your Life - Share the Love

"Think of your life as a series of doors you try to unlock and open to experience more of what you deserve most today. These doors swing wide open."

– Vic Conant / Chairman of the Board, Nightingale-Conant

As we start to wrap up our man meeting, I would like to thank you for hanging out with us. Hopefully you enjoyed yourself and learned as much as we did. I always have a good time hanging out with the guys and swapping stories and information. If you did learn something while spending time with us, consider sharing it with your friends. If you learned some effective techniques to make the woman you desire fall in love with you, tell your buddies so they can become as happy as you. I also encourage you to visit my website at www.findinghersweetspot.com where you can share your ideas and see what interesting thoughts other friends posted. Life is a continuous learning process, and the more we learn the easier it is to achieve our goals.

Our waitress Roxanne was very kind and patiently put up with our guy shenanigans this evening. So we must show our appreciation for her excellent service and personality which made our evening even more fun. We will make certain to leave her a generous tip. As we are waiting for our check I would like to interject some last minute thoughts. This step is called *share the love* for a reason. Part of achieving our goals is showing appreciation. We show appreciation for what we have in our lives already and for those people around us who make our lives better. Many people believe the universe will not give us more then we can handle. If you can't effectively handle what you have now, you won't get any more. So a great way to show appreciation is to share. There is a saying I heard many years ago that has stuck with me. "If you see someone without a smile, give them yours." I know this may sound a little corny, but you would be amazed how effective it is. I smile at people wherever I go. I especially smile at the people who seem particularly surly, shy or generally unfriendly. You would be amazed at how many people will smile back. You can physically notice how they soften and become more at ease. It is almost a conditioned response for people to reciprocate when you do something nice *to* them. But when you share something that makes someone else's life better, it will come back to you tenfold.

Part of being successful and achieving your goals is being a good receiver. In this case, it would be about receiving love. You made the woman of your dreams fall in love with you. Now you have to be willing to receive it. Some people subconsciously or consciously feel they are not deserving of love, money, success or many other good things in life. Do you feel uncomfortable when you get a compliment, someone offers to pay for your meal, or offers you affection? This actually happens more often and to more people than you would think. We are all deserving of what we want in life. Remember the story we tell ourselves? If you are one of those people who has trouble being a good receiver of the gifts life gives to you, you need to change your story. If you are not willing to receive what is being offered, you will miss out on many important opportunities in life. Let's say you are a very generous person. You feel joy when you give to others. Maybe it's sharing your financial gains, making a friend feel better if they are feeling down, or making your girlfriend happy by taking her out to dinner. By not giving others the opportunity to be generous toward you, it is taking away their opportunity to do something that makes them feel good.

I went through most of life always paying for the woman I was with. They would offer to pay for dinner, a movie or something else we were doing, but I always refused. One day a woman I was dating got furious with me. We were about to walk into a restaurant and she said "Tonight I am going to buy you dinner." I responded with "That is very sweet of you to offer but…" She quickly interrupted me and informed me that she just wanted to go home. I was mystified at why she was angry at all, much less so intensely angry she wanted to leave. I asked her what was wrong. She told me she was tired of me not allowing her to do anything nice for me. She explained how when she tries to show me that she cares about me and wants to do something nice for me, I always refuse. It would make her feel good to express to me how she feels, but I wasn't allowing her to. I thought about this for a few moments and discovered she was right. I always liked to make my girlfriends and my friends feel special, but it made me feel uncomfortable for them to make me feel special. That night I let her pay for my dinner. She practically glowed while paying the check and excitedly told the waiter how she finally got to take me out for dinner. The waiter looked a little confused but went with the flow. For the rest of the night she was so happy and was very grateful to me for giving her that opportunity. Who knew allowing her to buy me dinner would make her happy? I was grateful to have learned this lesson. I shared it with some friends who confirmed my behavior. Now I give others the opportunity to feel as good as I do by letting them do something nice for me.

After you are done reading this step this you might want to get a pen and paper and take a few moments to start writing down some of your goals. It is a great method to be able to focus on what you really want. Be sure to revisit them regularly. These goals can and should include ALL areas of your life, not just your love life. If you are going to take the steps to improve your love life, why not work on some other areas you would like to improve as well? We all have areas in our lives we would like to improve. Why not start now? It also helps to share some of these goals with a close friend. It helps keep you accountable when they ask you about your progress. It keeps you taking positive forward steps because you know they are going to ask. Or if your goal is to meet someone, perhaps they are willing to help by joining you in some activities. Having a good wingman is always a good thing. Bob offered to be my wingman once; little did I know he meant the appetizers. I was left within a group of women out for the evening while he went back to the table for "the wings." Thanks Bob.

Remember, we either choose what we do in our lives or someone else will end up choosing for us. Not taking action is taking an action. It is allowing someone else to make decisions for us. Regardless of our action or inaction, we will have to deal with the consequences. My sister laughed at me when I told her I enjoy sitting down and paying my bills. She asked "Why would you enjoy paying bills?" My response was simple, "Because I can." I am grateful every month that I can afford to pay those bills. There was a time in my life when I struggled to keep the utilities on in my apartment. On occasion, I was not so successful. So, if I don't pay the bills, someone else gets to decide to shut my power off. If I choose not to maintain my car, someone else gets to decide how much it costs to fix it. And if I don't decide to take positive actions in my life, I will not achieve my goals and always be at the mercy of a life that does not make me happy.

Think back to when you were a kid in grade school on summer break. The summer seemed to last longer. The school year seemed to last forever. As we get older time seems to go by faster and faster. We hesitate to do the things we want to do. You get too busy with your job, family and playing with electronic devices. Before you know it a huge chunk of time has passed and you are wondering what you did with the time and what you accomplished. Most people let years and years go by before they wake up and smell their discontent. You don't have to be that guy! Find Her Sweet Spot. Woo your woman, woo yourself and woo your life! Woo hoo!

We all hate to leave at the end of the guy's night out, but we get up and head for the door. We take turns bro hugging each one of our crew. Since you joined our crew, consider yourself bro hugged from us all. We are always happy for the time we spend together and looking forward to the next time we see each other. Does the waitress feel the same way? Yeeaah, she digs us.

I haven't told the guys yet, but I have managed to work my way into the ladies' night out. The girlfriends, wives and some female friends of my crew are allowing me to sit in on their girl's night out. So keep an eye out for my next book in the **Sweet Spot Series**. You can find it at findinghersweetspot.com or wrightwaypubling.com. I am going to share honest viewpoints, advice and stories with the women. If you found this book helpful, you can get the women in your life a copy of the new book when it's released. I promise it will be beneficial for both of you.

CONCLUSION

Dear Reader,

I have been studying personal growth, human behavior and relationship building skills for over twenty years. As an entrepreneur and corporate affiliate it has been vital to understand why people think, feel and respond in a certain manner. From a personal perspective I have had the opportunity to improve my life and the relationships with those around me.

The steps in this book will help you gain better insight into yourself, women and intimate relationships. Many of these techniques can be used to improve other relationships also (friends, family, coworkers). Some parts of these steps are designed to help you achieve your personal goals as well. The results will lead to a happier more successful life for you and an exciting passionate relationship with the woman you love.

Enjoy a Great Life and Great Relationships.

Sincerely,

William

WILLIAM WRIGHT

www.ingramcontent.com/pod-product-compliance
Lightning Source LLC
Chambersburg PA
CBHW061439040426
42450CB00007B/1131